ESSENTIALS
of Financial Risk Management

Essentials Series

The Essentials Series was created for busy business advisory and corporate professionals. The books in this series were designed so that these busy professionals can
quickly acquire knowledge and skills in core business areas.

Each book provides need-to-have fundamentals for those professionals who must:

- Get up to speed quickly, because they have been promoted to a new
  position or have broadened their responsibility scope

- Manage a new functional area

- Brush up on new developments in their area of responsibility

- Add more value to their company or clients

Other books in this series include:

Essentials of Accounts Payable, Mary S. Schaeffer

Essentials of Balanced Scorecard, Mohan Nair

Essentials of Capacity Management, Reginald Tomas Yu-Lee

Essentials of Capital Budgeting, James Sagner

Essentials of Cash Flow, H. A. Schaeffer, Jr.

Essentials of Corporate Performance Measurement, George T. Friedlob,
Lydia L. F. Schleifer, and Franklin J. Plewa, Jr.

Essentials of Cost Management, Joe and Catherine Stenzel

Essentials of Credit, Collections, and Accounts Receivable, Mary S. Schaeffer

Essentials of CRM: A Guide to Customer Relationship Management,
Bryan Bergeron

Essentials of Financial Analysis, George T. Friedlob and Lydia L. F. Schleifer

Essentials of Financial Risk Management, Karen A. Horcher

Essentials of Intellectual Property, Paul J. Lerner and Alexander I. Poltorak

Essentials of Knowledge Management, Bryan Bergeron

Essentials of Patents, Andy Gibbs and Bob DeMatteis

Essentials of Payroll Management and Accounting, Steven M. Bragg

Essentials of Shared Services, Bryan Bergeron

Essentials of Supply Chain Management, Michael Hugos

Essentials of Trademarks and Unfair Competition, Dana Shilling

Essentials of Treasury, Karen A. Horcher

Essentials of Managing Corporate Cash, Michele Allman-Ward and
James Sagner

Essentials of XBRL, Bryan Bergeron

For more information on any of these titles, please visit www.wiley.com.

ESSENTIALS
of Financial Risk Management

Karen A. Horcher

WILEY

John Wiley & Sons, Inc.

Published by John Wiley & Sons, Inc., Hoboken, New Jersey.

Published simultaneously in Canada.

For general information on our other products and services, or technical support, please contact our Customer Care Department within the United States at 800-762-2974, outside the United States at 317-572-3993, or fax 317-572-4002.

Wiley also publishes its books in a variety of electronic formats. Some content that appears in print may not be available in electronic books.

For more information about Wiley products, visit our Web site at www.wiley.com.

Library of Congress Cataloging-in-Publication Data:

Horcher, Karen A.
  Essentials of financial risk management / Karen A. Horcher.
    p. cm. — (Essentials series)
  Includes index.
  ISBN-13 978-0-471-70616-8 (pbk.)
  ISBN-10 0-471-70616-7 (pbk.)
  1. Risk management. 2. Financial futures. I. Title. II. Series.
  HD61.H58 2005
  658.15'5—dc22

                                                                    2004029115

Printed in the United States of America

10   9   8   7   6   5   4   3   2   1

For Uncle Jimmy

Contents

Preface

Financial markets are a fascinating reflection of the people behind them. Usually interesting, occasionally irrational, markets take on a life of their own, moving farther and faster than models predict and sometimes concluding with events that are theoretically unlikely.

There is tremendous value in a qualitative, as well as a quantitative, approach to risk management. Risk management cannot be reduced to a simple checklist or mechanistic process. In risk management, the ability to question and contemplate different outcomes is a distinct advantage.

This book is intended for the business or finance professional to bridge a gap between an overview of financial risk management and the many technical, though excellent, resources that are often beyond the level required by a nonspecialist.

Since the subject of financial risk management is both wide and deep, this volume is necessarily selective. Financial risk is covered from the top down, to foster an understanding of the risks and the methods often used to manage those risks.

The reader will find additional sources of information in the appendix. Of course, no book can serve as an alternative to professionals who can provide up-to-the-minute guidance on the many legal, financial, and technical challenges associated with risk management.

Acknowledgments

My approach to risk is unavoidably influenced by my experience as a trader. I had the good fortune to be in a good place at the right time and to learn from others who willingly shared their experience. I am most grateful to the many people who have offered me a helping hand, encouragement, or inspiration along the way, including my clients.

My appreciation goes to Bernice Miedzinski and Melanie Rupp for their helpful insight and perspectives, and to Stephanie Sharp for her support. Many thanks to Sheck for providing me with the opportunity. Special thanks are due to Paul for his encouragement and strength, and to Ashley.

CHAPTER 1

What Is Financial Risk Management?

After reading this chapter you will be able to

- Describe the financial risk management process
- Identify key factors that affect interest rates, exchange rates, and commodity prices
- Appreciate the impact of history on financial markets

Although financial risk has increased significantly in recent years, risk and risk management are not contemporary issues. The result of increasingly global markets is that risk may originate with events thousands of miles away that have nothing to do with the domestic market. Information is available instantaneously, which means that change, and subsequent market reactions, occur very quickly.

The economic climate and markets can be affected very quickly by changes in exchange rates, interest rates, and commodity prices. Counterparties can rapidly become problematic. As a result, it is important to ensure financial risks are identified and managed appropriately. Preparation is a key component of risk management.

What Is Risk?

Risk provides the basis for opportunity. The terms *risk* and *exposure* have subtle differences in their meaning. Risk refers to the probability of loss, while exposure is the possibility of loss, although they are often used interchangeably. Risk arises as a result of exposure.

Exposure to financial markets affects most organizations, either directly or indirectly. When an organization has financial market exposure, there is a possibility of loss but also an opportunity for gain or profit. Financial market exposure may provide strategic or competitive benefits.

Risk is the likelihood of losses resulting from events such as changes in market prices. Events with a low probability of occurring, but that may result in a high loss, are particularly troublesome because they are often not anticipated. Put another way, risk is the probable variability of returns.

Potential Size of Loss	Probability of Loss
Potential for Large Loss	High Probability of Occurrence
Potential for Small Loss	Low Probability of Occurrence

Since it is not always possible or desirable to eliminate risk, understanding it is an important step in determining how to manage it. Identifying exposures and risks forms the basis for an appropriate financial risk management strategy.

How Does Financial Risk Arise?

Financial risk arises through countless transactions of a financial nature, including sales and purchases, investments and loans, and various other business activities. It can arise as a result of legal transactions, new projects, mergers and acquisitions, debt financing, the energy component of costs, or through the activities of management, stakeholders, competitors, foreign governments, or weather.

When financial prices change dramatically, it can increase costs, reduce revenues, or otherwise adversely impact the profitability of an organization. Financial fluctuations may make it more difficult to plan and budget, price goods and services, and allocate capital.

There are three main sources of financial risk:

1. Financial risks arising from an organization's exposure to changes in market prices, such as interest rates, exchange rates, and commodity prices

2. Financial risks arising from the actions of, and transactions with, other organizations such as vendors, customers, and counterparties in derivatives transactions

3. Financial risks resulting from internal actions or failures of the organization, particularly people, processes, and systems

These are discussed in more detail in subsequent chapters.

What Is Financial Risk Management?

Financial risk management is a process to deal with the uncertainties resulting from financial markets. It involves assessing the financial risks facing an organization and developing management strategies consistent with internal priorities and policies. Addressing financial risks proactively may provide an organization with a competitive advantage. It also ensures that management, operational staff, stakeholders, and the board of directors are in agreement on key issues of risk.

Managing financial risk necessitates making organizational decisions about risks that are acceptable versus those that are not. The passive strategy of taking no action is the acceptance of all risks by default.

Organizations manage financial risk using a variety of strategies and products. It is important to understand how these products and strategies work to reduce risk within the context of the organization's risk tolerance and objectives.

Strategies for risk management often involve derivatives. Derivatives are traded widely among financial institutions and on organized exchanges. The value of derivatives contracts, such as futures, forwards, options, and

Notable Quote

"Whether we like it or not, mankind now has a completely integrated, international financial and informational marketplace capable of moving money and ideas to any place on this planet in minutes."

Source: Walter Wriston of Citibank, in a speech to the International Monetary Conference, London, June 11, 1979.

swaps, is derived from the price of the underlying asset. Derivatives trade on interest rates, exchange rates, commodities, equity and fixed income securities, credit, and even weather.

The products and strategies used by market participants to manage financial risk are the same ones used by speculators to increase leverage and risk. Although it can be argued that widespread use of derivatives increases risk, the existence of derivatives enables those who wish to reduce risk to pass it along to those who seek risk and its associated opportunities.

The ability to estimate the likelihood of a financial loss is highly desirable. However, standard theories of probability often fail in the analysis of financial markets. Risks usually do not exist in isolation, and the interactions of several exposures may have to be considered in developing an understanding of how financial risk arises. Sometimes, these interactions are difficult to forecast, since they ultimately depend on human behavior.

The process of financial risk management is an ongoing one. Strategies need to be implemented and refined as the market and requirements change. Refinements may reflect changing expectations about market rates, changes to the business environment, or changing international political conditions, for example. In general, the process can be summarized as follows:

- Identify and prioritize key financial risks.

- Determine an appropriate level of risk tolerance.

- Implement risk management strategy in accordance with policy.

- Measure, report, monitor, and refine as needed.

Diversification

For many years, the riskiness of an asset was assessed based only on the variability of its returns. In contrast, modern portfolio theory considers not only an asset's riskiness, but also its contribution to the overall riskiness of the portfolio to which it is added. Organizations may have an opportunity to reduce risk as a result of risk diversification.

In portfolio management terms, the addition of individual components to a portfolio provides opportunities for diversification, within limits. A diversified portfolio contains assets whose returns are dissimilar, in other words, weakly or negatively correlated with one another. It is useful to think of the exposures of an organization as a portfolio and consider the impact of changes or additions on the potential risk of the total.

Diversification is an important tool in managing financial risks. Diversification among counterparties may reduce the risk that unexpected events adversely impact the organization through defaults. Diversification among investment assets reduces the magnitude of loss if one issuer fails. Diversification of customers, suppliers, and financing sources reduces the possibility that an organization will have its business adversely affected by changes outside management's control. Although the risk of loss still exists, diversification may reduce the opportunity for large adverse outcomes.

TIPS & TECHNIQUES

Hedging and Correlation

Hedging is the business of seeking assets or events that offset, or have weak or negative correlation to, an organization's financial exposures.

Correlation measures the tendency of two assets to move, or not move, together. This tendency is quantified by a coefficient between −1 and +1. Correlation of +1.0 signifies perfect positive correlation and means that two assets can be expected to move together. Correlation of −1.0 signifies perfect negative correlation, which means that two assets can be expected to move together but in opposite directions.

The concept of *negative correlation* is central to hedging and risk management. Risk management involves pairing a financial exposure with an instrument or strategy that is negatively correlated to the exposure.

A long futures contract used to hedge a short underlying exposure employs the concept of negative correlation. If the price of the underlying (short) exposure begins to rise, the value of the (long) futures contract will also increase, offsetting some or all of the losses that occur. The extent of the protection offered by the hedge depends on the degree of negative correlation between the two.

Risk Management Process

The process of financial risk management comprises strategies that enable an organization to manage the risks associated with financial markets. Risk management is a dynamic process that should evolve with an organization and its business. It involves and impacts many parts of an organization including treasury, sales, marketing, legal, tax, commodity, and corporate finance.

The risk management process involves both internal and external analysis. The first part of the process involves identifying and prioritizing the financial risks facing an organization and understanding their relevance. It may be necessary to examine the organization and its products, management, customers, suppliers, competitors, pricing, industry trends, balance sheet structure, and position in the industry. It is also necessary to consider stakeholders and their objectives and tolerance for risk.

Once a clear understanding of the risks emerges, appropriate strategies can be implemented in conjunction with risk management policy. For example, it might be possible to change where and how business is done, thereby reducing the organization's exposure and risk. Alternatively, existing exposures may be managed with derivatives. Another strategy for managing risk is to accept all risks and the possibility of losses.

There are three broad alternatives for managing risk:

1. Do nothing and actively, or passively by default, accept all risks.

2. Hedge a portion of exposures by determining which exposures can and should be hedged.

3. Hedge all exposures possible.

Measurement and reporting of risks provides decision makers with information to execute decisions and monitor outcomes, both before and after strategies are taken to mitigate them. Since the risk management process is ongoing, reporting and feedback can be used to refine the system by modifying or improving strategies.

An active decision-making process is an important component of risk management. Decisions about potential loss and risk reduction provide a forum for discussion of important issues and the varying perspectives of stakeholders.

Factors that Impact Financial Rates and Prices

Financial rates and prices are affected by a number of factors. It is essential to understand the factors that impact markets because those factors, in turn, impact the potential risk of an organization.

Factors that Affect Interest Rates

Interest rates are a key component in many market prices and an important economic barometer. They are comprised of the real rate plus a component for expected inflation, since inflation reduces the purchasing power of a lender's assets. The greater the term to maturity, the greater the uncertainty. Interest rates are also reflective of supply and demand for funds and credit risk.

Interest rates are particularly important to companies and governments because they are the key ingredient in the cost of capital. Most companies and governments require debt financing for expansion and capital projects. When interest rates increase, the impact can be significant on borrowers. Interest rates also affect prices in other financial markets, so their impact is far-reaching.

Other components to the interest rate may include a risk premium to reflect the creditworthiness of a borrower. For example, the threat of political or sovereign risk can cause interest rates to rise, sometimes substantially, as investors demand additional compensation for the increased risk of default.

Factors that influence the level of market interest rates include:

- Expected levels of inflation

- General economic conditions

- Monetary policy and the stance of the central bank

- Foreign exchange market activity

- Foreign investor demand for debt securities

- Levels of sovereign debt outstanding

- Financial and political stability

Yield Curve

The yield curve is a graphical representation of yields for a range of terms to maturity. For example, a yield curve might illustrate yields for maturity from one day (overnight) to 30-year terms. Typically, the rates are zero coupon government rates.

Since current interest rates reflect expectations, the yield curve provides useful information about the market's expectations of future interest rates. Implied interest rates for forward-starting terms can be calculated using the information in the yield curve. For example, using rates for one- and two-year maturities, the expected one-year interest rate beginning in one year's time can be determined.

The shape of the yield curve is widely analyzed and monitored by market participants. As a gauge of expectations, it is often considered to be a predictor of future economic activity and may provide signals of a pending change in economic fundamentals.

The yield curve normally slopes upward with a positive slope, as lenders/investors demand higher rates from borrowers for longer lending terms. Since the chance of a borrower default increases with term to maturity, lenders demand to be compensated accordingly.

Interest rates that make up the yield curve are also affected by the expected rate of inflation. Investors demand at least the expected rate of inflation from borrowers, in addition to lending and risk components. If investors expect future inflation to be higher, they will demand greater premiums for longer terms to compensate for this uncertainty.

Predicting Change

Indicators that predict changes in economic activity in advance of a slowdown are extremely useful. The *yield curve* may be one such forecasting tool. Changes in consensus forecasts and actual short-term interest rates, as well as the index of leading indicators, have been used as warning signs of a change in the direction of the economy. Some studies have found that, historically at least, a good predictor of changes in the economy one year to 18 months forward has been the shape of the yield curve.

As a result, the longer the term, the higher the interest rate (all else being equal), resulting in an upward-sloping yield curve.

Occasionally, the demand for short-term funds increases substantially, and short-term interest rates may rise above the level of longer-term interest rates. This results in an inversion of the yield curve and a downward slope to its appearance. The high cost of short-term funds detracts from gains that would otherwise be obtained through investment and expansion and make the economy vulnerable to slowdown or recession. Eventually, rising interest rates slow the demand for both short-term and long-term funds. A decline in all rates and a return to a normal curve may occur as a result of the slowdown.

Theories of Interest Rate Determination

Several major theories have been developed to explain the term structure of interest rates and the resulting yield curve:

- Expectations theory suggests forward interest rates are representative of expected future interest rates. As a result, the shape of the yield curve and the term structure of rates are reflective of the market's aggregate expectations.

- Liquidity theory suggests that investors will choose longer-term maturities if they are provided with additional yield that compensates them for lack of liquidity. As a result, liquidity theory supports that forward interest rates possess a liquidity premium and an interest rate expectation component.

- Preferred habitat hypothesis suggests that investors who usually prefer one maturity horizon over another can be convinced to change maturity horizons given an appropriate premium. This suggests that the shape of the yield curve depends on the policies of market participants.

- Market segmentation theory suggests that different investors have different investment horizons that arise from the nature of their business or as a result of investment restrictions. These prevent them from dramatically changing maturity dates to take advantage of temporary opportunities in interest rates. Companies that have a long investment time horizon will therefore be less interested in taking advantage of opportunities at the short end of the curve.

Factors that Affect Foreign Exchange Rates

Foreign exchange rates are determined by supply and demand for currencies. Supply and demand, in turn, are influenced by factors in the economy, foreign trade, and the activities of international investors. Capital flows, given their size and mobility, are of great importance in determining exchange rates.

Factors that influence the level of interest rates also influence exchange rates among floating or market-determined currencies. Currencies are very sensitive to changes or anticipated changes in interest rates and to sovereign risk factors. Some of the key drivers that affect exchange rates include:

- Interest rate differentials net of expected inflation
- Trading activity in other currencies
- International capital and trade flows
- International institutional investor sentiment
- Financial and political stability
- Monetary policy and the central bank
- Domestic debt levels (e.g., debt-to-GDP ratio)
- Economic fundamentals

Key Drivers of Exchange Rates

When trade in goods and services with other countries was the major determinant of exchange-rate fluctuations, market participants monitored trade flow statistics closely for information about the currency's future direction. Today, capital flows are also very important and are monitored closely.

When other risk issues are considered equal, those currencies with higher short-term real interest rates will be more attractive to international investors than lower interest rate currencies. Currencies that are more attractive to foreign investors are the beneficiaries of capital mobility.

The freedom of capital that permits an organization to invest and divest internationally also permits capital to seek a safe, opportunistic return. Some currencies are particularly attractive during times of financial turmoil. Safe-haven currencies have, at various times, included the Swiss franc, the Canadian dollar, and the U.S. dollar.

Foreign exchange forward markets are tightly linked to interest markets. In freely traded currencies, traders arbitrage between the forward currency markets and the interest rate markets, ensuring interest rate parity.

Theories of Exchange Rate Determination

Several theories have been advanced to explain how exchange rates are determined:

- Purchasing power parity, based in part on "the law of one price," suggests that exchange rates are in equilibrium when the prices of goods and services (excluding mobility and other issues) in different countries are the same. If local prices increase more than prices in another country for the same product, the local currency would be expected to decline in value vis-à-vis its foreign counterpart, presuming no change in the structural relationship between the countries.

- The balance of payments approach suggests that exchange rates result from trade and capital transactions that, in turn, affect the balance of payments. The equilibrium exchange rate is reached when both internal and external pressures are in equilibrium.

- The monetary approach suggests that exchange rates are determined by a balance between the supply of, and demand for, money. When the money supply in one country increases compared with its trading partners, prices should rise and the currency should depreciate.

- The asset approach suggests that currency holdings by foreign investors are chosen based on factors such as real interest rates, as compared with other countries.

Factors that Affect Commodity Prices

Physical commodity prices are influenced by supply and demand. Unlike financial assets, the value of commodities is also affected by attributes such as physical quality and location.

Commodity supply is a function of production. Supply may be reduced if problems with production or delivery occur, such as crop failures or labor disputes. In some commodities, seasonal variations of supply and demand are usual and shortages are not uncommon.

Demand for commodities may be affected if final consumers are able to obtain substitutes at a lower cost. There may also be major shifts in consumer taste over the long term if there are supply or cost issues.

Commodity traders are sensitive to the inclination of certain commodity prices to vary according to the stage of the economic cycle. For example, base metals prices may rise late in the economic cycle as a result of increased economic demand and expansion. Prices of these commodities are monitored as a form of leading indicator.

Commodity prices may be affected by a number of factors, including:

- Expected levels of inflation, particularly for precious metals

- Interest rates

- Exchange rates, depending on how prices are determined

- General economic conditions

- Costs of production and ability to deliver to buyers

- Availability of substitutes and shifts in taste and consumption patterns

- Weather, particularly for agricultural commodities and energy

- Political stability, particularly for energy and precious metals

Financial Risk Management: A Selective History

No discussion of financial risk management is complete without a brief look at financial market history. Although this history is by no means complete, it illustrates events and highlights of the past several hundred years.

Early Markets

Financial derivatives and markets are often considered to be modern developments, but in many cases they are not. The earliest trading involved commodities, since they are very important to human existence. Long before industrial development, informal commodities markets operated to facilitate the buying and selling of products.

Marketplaces have existed in small villages and larger cities for centuries, allowing farmers to trade their products for other items of value. These marketplaces are the predecessors of modern exchanges. The later development of formalized futures markets enabled producers and buyers to guarantee a price for sales and purchases. The ability to trade product and guarantee a price was particularly important in markets where products had limited life, or where products were too bulky to transport to market often.

Forward contracts were used by Flemish traders at medieval trade fairs as early as the twelfth century, where *lettres de faire* were used to specify future delivery. Other reports of contractual agreements date back to Phoenician times. Futures contracts also facilitated trading in prized tulip bulbs in seventeenth-century Amsterdam during the infamous *tulip mania* era.

In seventeenth-century Japan, rice was an important commodity. As growers began to trade rice tickets for cash, a secondary market began to flourish. The Dojima rice futures market was established in the commerce center of Osaka in 1688 with 1,300 registered rice traders. Rice dealers could sell futures in advance of a harvest in anticipation of lower prices, or alternatively buy rice futures contracts if it looked as though the harvest might be poor and prices high. Rice tickets represented either warehoused rice or rice that would be harvested in the future.

Trading at the Dojima market was accompanied by a slow-burning rope in a box suspended from the roof. The day's trading ended when the rope stopped burning. The day's trading might be canceled, however, if there were no trading price when the rope stopped burning or if it expired early.

North American Developments

In North America, development of futures markets is also closely tied to agricultural markets, in particular the grain markets of the nineteenth century. Volatility in the price of grain made business challenging for both growers and merchant buyers.

The Chicago Board of Trade (CBOT), formed in 1848, was the first organized futures exchange in the United States. Its business was nonstandardized grain forward contracts. Without a central clearing organization, however, some participants defaulted on their contracts, leaving others unhedged.

In response, the CBOT developed futures contracts with standardized terms and the requirement of a performance bond in 1865. These were the first North American futures contracts. The contracts permitted farmers to fix a price for their grain sales in advance of delivery on a standardized basis. For the better part of a century, North American futures trading revolved around the grain industry, where large-scale production and consumption, combined with expense of transport and storage, made grain an ideal futures market commodity.

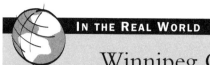

IN THE REAL WORLD

Winnipeg Commodity Exchange

Geographically central cities like Winnipeg and Chicago were attractive trading locations for agricultural commodities due to their proximity to transportation and growing regions. In Canada, the Winnipeg Commodity Exchange was formed in 1887 by ten enterprising local grain merchants. By 1928, Canada was producing nearly half of the world's grain supply, and Winnipeg became the foremost grain market and the benchmark for world grain prices. Though Winnipeg later had the distinction of introducing the first gold futures contract in 1972, its 400-ounce contract size became unwieldy once gold prices began their rapid ascent.

Turbulence in Financial Markets

In the 1970s, turbulence in world financial markets resulted in several important developments. Regional war and conflict, persistent high interest rates and inflation, weak equities markets, and agricultural crop failures produced major price instability.

Amid this volatility came the introduction of floating exchange rates. Shortly after the United States ended gold convertibility of the U.S. dollar, the Bretton Woods agreement effectively ended and the currencies of major industrial countries moved to floating rates. Although the currency market is a virtual one, it is the largest market, and London remains the most important center for foreign exchange trading.

Trading in interest rate futures began in the 1970s, reflecting the increasingly volatile markets. The New York Mercantile Exchange (NYMEX) introduced the first energy futures contract in 1978 with heating oil futures. These contracts provided a way for hedgers to manage price risk. Other developments include the establishment of the Commodity Futures Trading Commission.

Automation and Growth

The first automated exchange began not in New York or in London but at the International Futures Exchange in Bermuda in 1984. Despite its attractive location and the foresight to automate, the exchange did not survive. However, for exchanges today, automation is often a key to survival. New resources are making their way into trading and electronic order matching systems, improving efficiency and reducing trading costs. Some exchanges are entirely virtual, replacing a physical trading floor with interconnected traders all over the world.

In October 1987, financial markets were tested in a massive equity market decline, most of which took place over a couple of days. Some major exchanges suffered single-day declines of more than 20 percent. Futures trading volumes skyrocketed and central banks pumped liquidity into the market, sending interest rates lower. At the CBOT, futures trading volumes were three times that of the New York Stock Exchange.

Later, some observers suggested that the futures markets had contributed to the panic by spooking investors. Exchanges subsequently implemented new price limits and tightened existing ones. Some traders credit leveraged futures traders with the eleventh-hour rebound in stock prices. The rally that began in the futures pits slowly spread to other markets, and depth and liquidity returned.

The lessons of 1987 were not lost on regulators and central banks. The financial market turbulence and events highlighted serious vulnerabilities in the financial system and concerns about systemic risk. In many cases, developments have taken years to coordinate internationally but have brought lasting impact. Some of these developments are discussed in Chapter 10.

IN THE REAL WORLD

The Plaza and the Louvre

In the early 1980s, high U.S. interest rates caused the U.S. dollar to rise sharply against the currencies of its major trading partners, such as the Deutsche mark and the Japanese yen. In 1985 the G-5 central banks (representing the United States, Germany, France, Great Britain, and Japan) agreed to stop the rise of the U.S. dollar through central bank coordinated intervention. The agreement became known as the Plaza Accord, after the landmark New York hotel where meetings were held.

The Plaza Accord was successful and the U.S. dollar declined substantially against other major currencies. As the U.S. dollar fell, foreign manufacturers' prices soared in the important U.S. export market.

Export manufacturers, such as major Japanese companies, were forced to slash profit margins to ensure their pricing remained competitive against the dramatic impact of exchange rates on the translated prices of their goods abroad.

Subsequent G-7 meetings between the original G-5, plus Canada and Italy, resulted in the 1987 Louvre Accord, the aim of which was to slow the fall of the U.S. dollar and foster monetary and fiscal policy cooperation among the G-7 countries.

New Era Finance

The 1990s brought the development of new derivatives products, such as weather and catastrophe contracts, as well as a broader acceptance of their use. Increased use of value–at–risk and similar tools for risk management improved risk management dialogue and methodologies.

Some spectacular losses punctuated the decade, including the fall of venerable Barings Bank, and major losses at Orange County (California), Daiwa Bank, and Long Term Capital Management. No longer were derivatives losses big news. In the new era of finance, the newsworthy losses were denominated in billions, rather than millions, of dollars.

In 1999, a new European currency, the euro, was adopted by Austria, Belgium, Finland, France, Germany, Ireland, Italy, Luxembourg, the Netherlands, Portugal, and Spain, and two years later, Greece. The move to a common currency significantly reduced foreign exchange risk for organizations doing business in Europe as compared with managing a dozen different currencies, and it sparked a wave of bank consolidations.

As the long equities bull market that had sustained through much of the previous decade lost steam, technology stocks reached a final spectacular top in 2000. Subsequent declines for some equities were worse than those of the post-1929 market, and the corporate failures that followed the boom made history. Shortly thereafter, the terrorist attacks of September 11, 2001 changed many perspectives on risk. Precious metals and energy commodities became increasingly attractive in an increasingly unsettled geopolitical environment.

New frontiers in the evolution of financial risk management include new risk modeling capabilities and trading in derivatives such as weather, environmental (pollution) credits, and economic indicators.

Summary

- Financial risk management is not a contemporary issue.
  Financial risk management has been a challenge for as long as there have been markets and price fluctuations.

- Financial risks arise from an organization's exposure to financial markets, its transactions with others, and its reliance on processes, systems, and people.

- To understand financial risks, it is useful to consider the factors that affect financial prices and rates, including interest rates, exchange rates, and commodities prices.

- Since financial decisions are made by humans, a little financial history is useful in understanding the nature of financial risk.

CHAPTER 2

Identifying Major Financial Risks

After reading this chapter you will be able to

- Evaluate the various financial risks that affect most organizations
- Describe how key market risks arise, such as interest rate risk, foreign exchange risk, and commodity price risk
- Consider the impact of related risks such as credit risk, operational risk, and systemic risk

Major market risks arise out of changes to financial market prices such as exchange rates, interest rates, and commodity prices. Major market risks are usually the most obvious type of financial risk that an organization faces. Major market risks include:

- Foreign exchange risk
- Interest rate risk
- Commodity price risk
- Equity price risk

Other important related financial risks include:

- Credit risk
- Operational risk

- Liquidity risk

- Systemic risk

The interactions of several risks can alter or magnify the potential impact to an organization. For example, an organization may have both commodity price risk and foreign exchange risk. If both markets move adversely, the organization may suffer significant losses as a result.

There are two components to assessing financial risk. The first component is an understanding of potential loss as a result of a particular rate or price change. The second component is an estimate of the probability of such an event occurring. These topics are explored in more detail in Chapter 9.

Interest Rate Risk

Interest rate risk arises from several sources, including:

- Changes in the level of interest rates (absolute interest rate risk)

- Changes in the shape of the yield curve (yield curve risk)

- Mismatches between exposure and the risk management strategies undertaken (basis risk)

Interest rate risk is the probability of an adverse impact on profitability or asset value as a result of interest rate changes. Interest rate risk affects many organizations, both borrowers and investors, and it particularly affects capital-intensive industries and sectors.

Changes affect borrowers through the cost of funds. For example, a corporate borrower that utilizes floating interest rate debt is exposed to rising interest rates that could increase the company's cost of funds. A

TIPS & TECHNIQUES

Fundamental
Market Terminology

Several fundamental market risks impact the value of assets or a portfolio. Although these risks are most often cited with respect to derivatives, most apply to nonderivatives exposures as well:

- *Absolute risk* (also known as delta risk) arises from exposure to changes in the price of the underlying asset or index.

- *Convexity risk* (also known as gamma risk) arises from exposure to the rate of change in the delta or duration of the underlying asset.

- *Volatility risk* (also known as vega risk) arises from exposure to changes in the implied volatility of the underlying security or asset.

- *Time decay risk* (also known as theta risk) arises from exposure to the passage of time.

- *Basis risk* (also known as correlation risk) arises from exposure to the extent of correlation of a hedge to the underlying assets or securities.

- *Discount rate risk* (also known as rho risk) arises from exposure to changes in interest rates used to discount future cash flows.

portfolio of fixed income securities has exposure to interest rates through both changes in yield and gains or losses on assets held.

Interest rate risk is discussed in more detail in Chapter 3.

Absolute Interest Rate Risk

Absolute interest rate risk results from the possibility of a directional, or up or down, change in interest rates. Most organizations monitor absolute interest rate risk in their risk assessments, due to both its visibility and its potential for affecting profitability.

From a borrower's perspective, rising interest rates might result in higher project costs and changes to financing or strategic plans. From an investor or lender perspective, a decline in interest rates results in lower interest income given the same investment, or alternatively, inadequate return on investments held. All else being equal, the greater the duration, the greater the impact of an interest rate change.

The most common method of hedging absolute interest rate risk is to match the duration of assets and liabilities, or replace floating interest rate borrowing or investments with fixed interest rate debt or investments. Another alternative is to hedge the interest rate risk with tools such as forward rate agreements, swaps, and interest rate caps, floors, and collars. Interest rate risk management is discussed in greater detail in Chapter 3.

Yield Curve Risk

Yield curve risk results from changes in the relationship between short- and long-term interest rates. In a normal interest rate environment, the yield curve has an upward-sloping shape to it. Longer-term interest rates are higher than shorter-term interest rates because of higher risk to the lender. The steepening or flattening of the yield curve changes the interest rate differential between maturities, which can impact borrowing and investment decisions and therefore profitability.

In an inverted yield curve environment, demand for short-term funds pushes short-term rates above long-term rates. The yield curve may appear inverted or flat across most maturities, or alternatively only in certain maturity segments. In such an environment, rates of longer terms to maturity may be impacted less than shorter terms to maturity. When there is a mismatch between an organization's assets and liabilities, yield curve risk should be assessed as a component of the organization's interest rate risk.

When the yield curve steepens, interest rates for longer maturities increase more than interest rates for shorter terms as demand for longer-term financing increases. Alternatively, short-term rates may drop while long-term rates remain relatively unchanged. A steeper yield curve results in a greater interest rate differential between short-term and long-term interest rates, which makes rolling debt forward more expensive. If a borrower is faced with a steep yield curve, there is a much greater cost to lock in borrowing costs for a longer term compared with a shorter term.

TIPS & TECHNIQUES

Trading the Yield Curve

Traders and strategists look for opportunities to trade the yield curve. They use various strategies to sell the interest rate differential between shorter- and longer-term interest rates when they feel that the yield curve is due to flatten. Similarly, they will buy the interest rate differential between shorter- and longer-term interest rates when they feel that the yield curve will steepen.

A flatter yield curve has a smaller gap between long- and short-term interest rates. This may occur as longer-term rates drop while short-term rates remain about the same. Alternatively, short-term demand for funds may ease, with little change to demand for longer-term funds. The flattening of the yield curve makes rolling debt forward cheaper because there is a smaller interest rate differential between maturity dates.

Yield curve swaps and strategies using products such as interest rate futures and forward rate agreements along the yield curve can take advantage of changes in the shape of the yield curve. The yield curve is a consideration whenever there is a mismatch between assets and liabilities.

Reinvestment or Refunding Risk

Reinvestment or refunding risk arises when interest rates at investment maturities (or debt maturities) result in funds being reinvested (or refinanced) at current market rates that are worse than forecast or anticipated. The inability to forecast the rollover rate with certainty has the potential to impact overall profitability of the investment or project.

For example, a short-term money market investor is exposed to the possibility of lower interest rates when current holdings mature. Investors who purchase callable bonds are also exposed to reinvestment risk. If callable bonds are called by the issuer because interest rates have fallen, the investor will have proceeds to reinvest at subsequently lower rates.

Similarly, a borrower that issues commercial paper to finance longer-term projects is exposed to the potential for higher rates at the rollover or refinancing date. As a result, matching funding duration to that of the underlying project reduces exposure to refunding risk.

Basis Risk

Basis risk is the risk that a hedge, such as a derivatives contract, does not move with the direction or magnitude to offset the underlying exposure, and it is a concern whenever there is a mismatch. Basis risk may occur when one hedging product is used as a proxy hedge for the underlying exposure, possibly because an appropriate hedge is expensive or impossible to find. The basis may narrow or widen, with potential for gains or losses as a result.

A narrower view of basis risk applies to futures prices, where basis is the difference between the cash and futures price. Over time, the relationship between the two prices may change, impacting the hedge. For example, if the price of a bond futures contract does not change in value in the same magnitude as the underlying interest rate exposure, the hedger may suffer a loss as a result.

Basis risk can also arise if prices are prevented from fully reflecting underlying market changes. This could potentially occur with some futures contracts, for example, where daily maximum price fluctuations are permitted. In the case of a significant intra-day market move, some futures prices may reach their limits and be prevented from moving the full intra-day price change.

Foreign Exchange Risk

Foreign exchange risk arises through transaction, translation, and economic exposures. It may also arise from commodity-based transactions where commodity prices are determined and traded in another currency. Foreign exchange risk is discussed in more detail in Chapter 4.

Transaction Exposure

Transaction risk impacts an organization's profitability through the income statement. It arises from the ordinary transactions of an organization, including purchases from suppliers and vendors, contractual payments in other currencies, royalties or license fees, and sales to customers in currencies other than the domestic one. Organizations that buy or sell products and services denominated in a foreign currency typically have transaction exposure.

Management of transaction risk can be an important determinant of competitiveness in a global economy. There are few corporations whose business is not affected, either directly or indirectly, by transaction risk.

Translation Exposure

Translation risk traditionally referred to fluctuations that result from the accounting translation of financial statements, particularly assets and liabilities on the balance sheet. Translation exposure results wherever assets, liabilities, or profits are translated from the operating currency into a reporting currency—for example, the reporting currency of the parent company.

From another perspective, translation exposure affects an organization by affecting the value of foreign currency balance sheet items such as accounts payable and receivable, foreign currency cash and deposits, and foreign currency debt. Longer-term assets and liabilities, such as those associated with foreign operations, are likely to be particularly impacted.

Foreign currency debt can also be considered a source of translation exposure. If an organization borrows in a foreign currency but has no offsetting currency assets or cash flows, increases in the value of the foreign currency vis-à-vis the domestic currency mean an increase in the translated market value of the foreign currency liability. This is discussed in more detail in Chapter 4.

Foreign Exchange Exposure from
Commodity Prices

Since many commodities are priced and traded internationally in U.S. dollars, exposure to commodities prices may indirectly result in foreign exchange exposure for non-U.S. organizations. Even when purchases or

IN THE REAL WORLD

Transaction Exposure

A small Canadian company receives service revenues from its international customers, mostly in U.S. dollars (USD). The company's costs, primarily research and development, are in Canadian dollars (CAD). The following exchange rates prevailed over a recent period:

Quarter	Revenues (USD)	Exchange Rate	Revenues (CAD)
Quarter 1 (actual)	$10,000,000	1.5218	$15,218,000
Quarter 2 (actual)	$10,000,000	1.4326	$14,326,000
Quarter 3 (actual)	$10,000,000	1.3328	$13,328,000
Quarter 4 (estimate)	$10,000,000	1.2910	$12,910,000

The difference in U.S. dollar revenue converted to Canadian dollars as a result of exchange rates from Quarter 1 to Quarter 3 is $1,890,000. It is unlikely that the company's costs would have similarly declined over the same period. This is a significant difference, and if the company's costs are unchanged, the company could suffer a loss as a result.

Of course, a company that is unhedged may also earn an unexpected profit should exchange rates move favorably.

sales are made in the domestic currency, exchange rates may be embedded in, and a component of, the commodity price.

In most cases, suppliers of commodities, like any other business, are forced to pass along changes in the exchange rate to their customers or suffer losses themselves.

IN THE REAL WORLD

Translation Exposure

The impact of exchange rates on unmanaged foreign currency debt can be significant. A U.S. company has funded its operations with a Canadian $10,000,000 liability. Without offsetting assets or cash flows, the value of the liability fluctuates with exchange rates. If the exchange rate moves from 0.7000 to 0.9000 (USD per CAD), it increases the company's liability by $2,000,000 (or 28 percent), as follows:

Exchange Rate	U.S. Dollar Liability
0.6500 USD/CAD	$ 6,500,000
0.7000	7,000,000
0.7500	7,500,000
0.8000	8,000,000
0.9000	9,000,000

By splitting the risk into currency and commodity components, an organization can assess both risks independently, determine an appropriate strategy for dealing with price and rate uncertainties, and obtain the most efficient pricing.

Protection through fixed rate contracts that provide exchange rate protection is beneficial if the exchange rate moves adversely. However, if the exchange rate moves favorably, the buyer might be better off without a fixed exchange rate. Without the benefit of hindsight, the hedger should understand both the exposure and the market to hedge when exposure involves combined commodity and currency rates.

Strategic Exposure

The location and activities of major competitors may be an important determinant of foreign exchange exposure. Strategic or economic exposure affects an organization's competitive position as a result of changes in exchange rates. Economic exposures, such as declining sales from international customers, do not show up on the balance sheet, though their impact appears in income statements.

For example, a firm whose domestic currency has appreciated dramatically may find its products are too expensive in international markets despite its efforts to reduce costs of production and minimize prices.

IN THE REAL WORLD

Commodity and Foreign Exchange Exposure

A manufacturer in Asia makes finished goods from plastic resins that it purchases from a domestic supplier. The domestic supplier prices its resins in the local currency, thus removing any uncertainties about the domestic currency price for the manufacturer.

However, the plastic resins have a commodity (petroleum) component, and therefore prices fluctuate to some degree with the price of oil. Since international oil prices are denominated in U.S. dollars, the Asian manufacturer has exposure to U.S. dollars indirectly through its purchase of raw materials, the price of which is based on a traded commodity priced in U.S. dollars. Of course, the manufacturer's actual exposure may depend on other factors and exposures.

The prices of goods exported by the firm's competitors, who are coincidentally located in a weak-currency environment, become cheaper by comparison without any action on their part.

Commodity Risk

Exposure to absolute price changes is the risk of commodity prices rising or falling. Organizations that produce or purchase commodities, or whose livelihood is otherwise related to commodity prices, have exposure to commodity price risk.

IN THE REAL WORLD

Strategic Exposure

Japanese exporters faced strategic exposure in the 1980s. As the value of the yen (JPY) appreciated dramatically against major trading partner currencies such as the U.S. dollar, Japanese exporters were faced with a tough choice between lowering profit margins (and price) to maintain foreign currency prices or losing market share in critical markets. In response, they aggressively cut costs, moved production to lower-cost offshore centers, and reduced profit margins, enabling them to maintain market share despite dramatic increases in the yen.

The following Japanese yen/U.S. dollar average spot exchange rates illustrate the dramatic moves that precipitated such action:

1985	238.60 JPY/USD
1986	168.50
1987	144.60
1988	128.15

Some commodities cannot be hedged because there is no effective forward market for the product. Generally, if a forward market exists, an options market may develop, either on an exchange or among institutions in the over-the-counter market.

In lieu of exchange-traded commodities markets, many commodity suppliers offer forward or fixed-price contracts to their clients. Financial institutions may offer similar products to clients, provided that a market exists for the product to permit the financial institution to hedge its own exposure. Financial institutions in some markets are limited by regulation to the types of commodity transactions they can undertake, though commodity derivatives may be permitted.

Commodity risk is discussed in more detail in Chapter 6.

Commodity Price Risk

Commodity price risk occurs when there is potential for changes in the price of a commodity that must be purchased or sold. Commodity exposure can also arise from non-commodity business if inputs or products and services have a commodity component.

Commodity price risk affects consumers and end-users such as manufacturers, governments, processors, and wholesalers. If commodity prices rise, the cost of commodity purchases increases, reducing profit from transactions.

Price risk also affects commodity producers. If commodity prices decline, the revenues from production also fall, reducing business income. Price risk is generally the greatest risk affecting the livelihood of commodity producers and should be managed accordingly.

Commodity prices may be set by local buyers and sellers in the domestic currency in order to facilitate local customer business. However, when transactions are conducted in the domestic currency for a commodity that is normally traded in another currency, such as U.S. dollars, the exchange rate will be a component of the total price for the commodity, and the currency exposure continues to be a consideration.

Some companies help their clients manage risk by offering domestic commodity prices. The company may fix the commodity price for a period of time or, alternatively, may pass along commodity price changes but allow customers to use a fixed exchange rate for calculating the domestic price. In the latter case, the supplier is effectively assuming the currency risk. Either scenario may be useful for small organizations or those that are only occasional buyers of a commodity and do not wish to manage the risk themselves.

Commodity Quantity Risk

Organizations have exposure to quantity risk through the demand for commodity assets. Although quantity is closely tied to price, quantity risk remains a risk with commodities since supply and demand are critical with physical commodities.

For example, if a farmer expects demand for product to be high and plans the season accordingly, there is a risk that the quantity the market demands will be less than has been produced. Demand may be less for a number of reasons, all of which are out of the control of the farmer. If so, the farmer may suffer a loss by being unable to sell all the product, even if prices do not change dramatically. This might be managed using a fixed price contract covering a minimum quantity of commodity as a hedge.

Contango and Backwardation

In a normal or contango market, the price of a commodity for future delivery is higher than the cash or spot price. The higher forward price accommodates the cost of owning the commodity from the trade date to the delivery date, including financing, insurance, and storage costs. Although the cash commodity buyer incurs these costs, the futures buyer does not. Therefore, the futures seller will usually demand a higher price to compensate for the higher costs incurred.

In general, the longer delivery is delayed, the more expensive the carrying charges. As delivery approaches, the forward or futures price will converge with the cash or spot price.

Markets do not always follow the normal pricing structure. When demand for cash or near-term delivery of a commodity exceeds supply, or there are supply problems, an inverted or backwardation market may result. Market participants bid up prices for immediate available supply, and prices for near-term delivery rise above prices for longer-term delivery.

At least one highly publicized corporate loss occurred as a result of a commodity market that had traded in backwardation for some time.

IN THE REAL WORLD

Backwardation

Heating oil, which is traded on the New York Mercantile Exchange (NYMEX), may exhibit backwardation near the end of the winter, as demand for heating oil is high for immediate delivery but low for future delivery when much less will be required. Those organizations that require heating oil for the winter months push up prices for immediate or short-term delivery. To speculate on future heating oil prices by buying and holding would require funding and storing the product until the following winter, an expensive proposition. As a result, there is less upward pressure on prices of longer-term contracts.

The company may have surmised that the backwardation pricing structure would continue, and it developed its hedging and trading strategies accordingly. When the market moved from backwardation back to a normal pricing structure, the company suffered significant losses.

Commodity Basis

The *basis* is the difference between the cash or spot price and the futures or forward price at any point in time. A shift in the basis, where the difference between cash prices and futures prices has changed, can mean additional gains or losses to hedgers. A forward or futures contract manages price risk but not necessarily basis risk.

Basis disappears as a futures contract reaches the delivery month and futures and spot prices converge, presuming that both the spot and futures prices represent identical product. Changes in the basis can play havoc with hedging.

IN THE REAL WORLD

Copper Prices

Prices of the following commodity (copper futures prices, cents per pound) display backwardation, with the April (near) delivery priced at 143.80 (U.S.) cents per pound, while the September delivery is priced at 128.00 cents per pound:

April	143.80
May	140.80
July	133.20
September	128.00
December	123.00

While the term basis has a specific meaning in futures markets, in the commodities markets it can also refer to differences due to the specifics of a particular commodity, such as its delivery point or local quality. Calculating a local basis involves adjusting market prices (such as those determined from futures exchanges) to reflect local characteristics and prices. The basis will change over time and represents a source of risk to a hedger if an imperfect hedge is used.

Special Risks

Commodities differ from financial contracts in several significant ways, primarily due to the fact that most have the potential to involve physical delivery. With notable exceptions such as electricity, commodities involve issues such as quality, delivery location, transportation, spoilage, shortages, and storability, and these issues affect price and trading activity.

In addition, market demand and the availability of substitutes may be important considerations. If prices of potential substitutes become attractive because a commodity is expensive or there are delivery difficulties, demand may shift, temporarily or in some cases, permanently.

Credit Risk

Credit risk is one of the most prevalent risks of finance and business. In general, credit risk is a concern when an organization is owed money or must rely on another organization to make a payment to it or on its behalf. The failure of a counterparty is less of an issue when the organization is not owed money on a net basis, although it depends to a certain degree on the legal environment and whether funds are owed on a net or aggregate basis on individual contracts. The deterioration of credit quality, such as that of a securities issuer, is also a source of risk through the reduced market value of securities that an organization might own.

Credit risk increases as time to expiry, time to settlement, or time to maturity increase. The move by international regulators to shorten settlement time for certain types of securities trades is an effort to reduce systemic risk, which in turn is based on the risk of individual market participants. It also increases in an environment of rising interest rates or poor economic fundamentals.

Organizations are exposed to credit risk through all business and financial transactions that depend on the payment or fulfillment of obligations of others. Credit risk that arises from exposure to a counterparty, such as in a derivatives transaction, is often known as counterparty risk. The subject of credit risk is discussed in more detail in Chapter 5.

Default Risk

Default risk arises from money owed, either through lending or investment, that the borrower is unable or unwilling to repay. The amount at risk is the defaulted amount, less any amount that can be recovered from the borrower. In many cases, the default amount is most or all of the advanced funds.

Counterparty Pre-Settlement Risk

Aside from settlement, counterparty exposure arises from the fact that if the counterparty defaults or otherwise does not fulfill its obligations under the terms of a contractual agreement, it might be necessary to enter into a replacement contract at far less favorable prices. The amount at risk is the net present value of future cash flows owed to the organization, presuming that no gross settlements would be required.

Potential future counterparty exposure is a probability estimate of potential future replacement cost if market rates move favorably for the hedger, which would result in a larger unrealized gain for the hedger and larger loss in the event of default. The amount at risk is the potential net present value of future cash flows owed to the organization.

Counterparty Settlement Risk

Settlement risk arises at the time that payments associated with a contract occur, particularly cross payments between counterparties. It has the potential to result in large losses because the entire amount of the payment between counterparties may be at risk if a counterparty fails during the settlement process. As a result, depending on the nature of the payment, the amount at risk may be significant because the notional amount could potentially be at risk. Because of the potential for loss, settlement risk is one of the key market risks that market participants and regulators have worked to reduce.

Settlement risk also exists with exchange-traded contracts. However, with exchange-traded contracts the counterparty is usually a clearinghouse or clearing corporation, rather than an individual institution.

Sovereign or Country Risk

Sovereign risk encompasses the legal, regulatory, and political exposures that affect international transactions and the movement of funds across borders. It arises through the actions of foreign governments and countries and can often result in significant financial volatility. Exposure to any nondomestic organization involves an analysis of the sovereign risk involved. In areas with political instability, sovereign risk is particularly important.

Concentration Risk

Concentration is a source of credit risk that applies to organizations with credit exposure in concentrated sectors. An organization that is poorly diversified, due to its industry or regional influences, has concentration risk. Concentration risk is most effectively managed with the addition of diversification, where possible.

Legal Risk

The risk that a counterparty is not legally permitted or able to enter into transactions, particularly derivatives transactions, is known as legal risk. The issue of legal risk has, in the past, arisen when a counterparty has suffered losses on outstanding derivatives contracts. A related issue is the legal structure of the counterparty, since many derivatives counterparties, for example, are wholly owned special-purpose subsidiaries.

The risk that an individual employed by an entity has sufficient authority to enter into a transaction, but that the entity itself does not have sufficient authority, has also caused losses in derivatives transactions. As a result, organizations should ensure that counterparties are legally authorized to enter into transactions.

Operational Risk

Operational risk arises from human error and fraud, processes and procedures, and technology and systems. Operational risk is one of the most significant risks facing an organization because of the varied opportunities for losses to occur and the fact that losses may be substantial when they occur. The subject of operational risk is discussed in more detail in Chapter 7.

Human Error and Fraud

Most business transactions involve human decision making and relationships. The size and volume of financial transactions makes the potential damage as a result of a large error or fraud quite significant.

Processes and Procedural Risk

Processes and procedural risk includes the risk of adverse consequences as the result of missing or ineffective processes, procedures, controls, or checks and balances. The use of inadequate controls is an example of a procedural risk.

Technology and Systems Risk

Technology and systems risk incorporates the operational risks arising from technology and systems that support the processes and transactions of an organization.

Other Types of Risk

Other types of risk include equity price risk, liquidity risk, and systemic risk, which are also of interest to financial market participants. Risks arising from embedded options are also a consideration.

Equity Price Risk

Equity price risk affects corporate investors with equities or other assets the performance of which is tied to equity prices. Firms may have equity exposure through pension fund investments, for example, where the return depends on a stream of dividends and favorable equity price movements to provide capital gains. The exposure may be to one stock, several stocks, or an industry or the market as a whole.

Equity price risk also affects companies' ability to fund operations through the sale of equity and equity-related securities. Equity risk is thus related to the ability of a firm to obtain sufficient capital or liquidity.

Liquidity Risk

Liquidity impacts all markets. It affects the ability to purchase or sell a security or obligation, either for hedging purposes or trading purposes, or alternatively to close out an existing position. Liquidity can also refer to an organization having the financial capacity to meet its short-term obligations.

Assessing liquidity is often subjective and involves qualitative assessments, but indicators of liquidity include number of financial institutions active in the market, average bid/ask spreads, trading volumes, and sometimes price volatility.

Although liquidity risk is difficult to measure or forecast, an organization can try to reduce transactions that are highly customized or unusual, or where liquidity depends on a small number of players and therefore is likely to be poor.

Another form of liquidity risk is the risk that an organization has insufficient liquidity to maintain its day-to-day operations. While revenues and sales may be sufficient for long-term growth, if short-term cash is insufficient, liquidity issues may require decisions that are detrimental to long-term growth.

Embedded Options

Embedded options are granted to securities holders or contract participants and provide them with certain rights. The granting of permission to buy or sell something is an option, and it has value. For example, the ability to repay a loan prior to its maturity is an option. If the borrower must pay a fee to repay the loan, the option has a cost. If the loan can be repaid without a fee, the option is free to the borrower, at least explicitly. The value of the option is likely to be at least partially embedded in the interest rate on the loan.

Embedded options commonly consist of redemption, call, or similar features in corporate debt securities. Embedded options may also exist in contractual pricing agreements with customers or suppliers or fixed-priced commodity contracts. The option holder is the party to whom the benefits accrue. The option grantor is the party that has an obligation as a result of the embedded option.

Embedded options are often ignored or not considered in risk management decisions. However, they affect the potential exposure of an organization and also offer risk management opportunities and therefore should be considered as such.

Systemic Risk

Systemic risk is the risk that the failure of a major financial institution could trigger a domino effect and many subsequent organizational failures, threatening the integrity of the financial system. Aside from practicing good risk management principles, systemic risk is difficult for an individual organization to mitigate.

Higher volumes, especially for foreign exchange and securities trading, increase liquidity, which has benefits to market participants. However, higher volumes also increase systemic risk. Systemic risk can also arise from technological failure or a major disaster. Some important initiatives are underway to mitigate systemic risk, and these are discussed in more detail in Chapter 10.

Summary

- Interest rate risk is the probability of an adverse impact as a result of interest rate fluctuations. Both borrowers and investors are affected by interest rate risk.

- Foreign exchange risk can arise from transaction exposure, translation exposure, strategic exposure, or as a result of commodity-based pricing. It may also have a competitive component.

- Commodities markets are unique in several ways. Risk management must take into account the basis and the tendency of commodities markets to exhibit backwardation.

- Other important risks, such as credit risk and operational risk, should also be managed in conjunction with market risks.

CHAPTER 3

Interest Rate Risk

After reading this chapter you will be able to

- Identify opportunities to reduce interest rate exposure
- Evaluate ways to manage interest rate risk with forward rate agreements, futures, and swaps
- Assess the use of interest rate options, including swaptions

Although the business of hedging usually involves derivatives, it is possible to rearrange activities to minimize interest rate exposure. Depending on its approach, an organization can supplement internal hedging strategies with interest rate derivatives such as forward rate agreements, futures, swaps, and options.

Interest rate derivatives may replace interest rate exposure with exposure to the performance of counterparties and raise other issues. Therefore, it is important to understand credit risk, which is discussed in more detail in Chapter 5.

Global Cash Netting

When an organization has cash flows in multiple currencies, some parts of the organization may have excess cash while others may need to draw down on available lines of credit. A cash forecast for specific currencies will enable surpluses and shortages to be forecast and managed

TIPS & TECHNIQUES

Exposure Reduction

Although it might be possible to manage interest rate exposure without derivatives, legal, tax, and regulatory ramifications must be taken into consideration, particularly in foreign countries or for cross-border transactions. These may prohibit such transactions or reduce or eliminate the benefit. The following techniques have been used to reduce interest rate exposure and the resulting need for derivatives:

- Global cash netting/inhouse bank

- Intercompany lending

- Embedded options in debt

- Changes to payment schedules

- Asset–liability management

more accurately. On a centralized basis, it may be possible to pool funds from divisions or subsidiaries and make them available to other parts of the organization.

Expert assistance is necessary in this area, since some countries prohibit or restrict intercompany transactions, including cash pooling. Tax and legal issues should be determined prior to engaging in such transactions.

Intercompany Lending

A longer-term approach to managing funding shortages and surpluses across an organization is intercompany lending. When one part of an organization requires long-term funding, and another part has excess cash available for investment purposes, the combination of the two may reduce interest costs and permit more control over the borrowing process. As with cash netting and pooling, expert assistance is necessary to ensure that legal, tax, and regulatory restrictions or prohibitions do not exist.

Embedded Options

The use of debt securities with features such as a call provision provides debt issuers with an alternative method for managing exposure to interest rates. Callable debt combines the debt component, which would typically otherwise not be callable, with the call provision, which provides an option to the issuer. If interest rates decline, the issuer can retire the higher-interest debt through the call provision and subsequently reissue lower-interest debt. The issuer will incur a cost for the call option through the call price premium or the coupon.

Changes to Payment Schedules

Changes to payment schedules may permit an organization to maintain cash balances for longer periods, reducing the need for funding and therefore exposure to interest rates:

- Changes to supplier/vendor payment schedules may permit a longer payment cycle, reducing the need for borrowing. Alternatively, payments may be made on behalf of other parts of the organization, which may permit netting to be used.

- Changes to customer payment schedules may increase the speed with which funds are collected, reducing the need for borrowing. Changing the methods used by customers to pay, such as encouraging electronic alternatives to paper checks, may also speed collections.

- Changes to contractual long-term payments, such as royalties and license agreements, to quarterly from annually, for example. A smaller, more regular payment may smooth the cash flow impact and make it easier to forecast, particularly in smaller organizations. Alternatively, an organization may find that changes to a less frequent basis may provide additional operating funds throughout the fiscal cycle.

Asset–Liability Management

In financial institutions, the management of assets and liabilities is a key requirement for managing interest rate risk. In some ways, it is also more predictable in financial institutions than in other organizations.

Asset–liability management involves the pairing or matching of assets (customer loans and mortgages in the case of a financial institution) and liabilities (customer deposits) so that changes in interest rates do not adversely impact the organization. This practice is commonly known as *gap management* and often involves duration matching.

Some nonfinancial companies have exposure to interest rate gaps through their own internal financing or programs. For example, companies may offer financing programs for their customers, while others provide financing internally on a project basis. Nonfinancial institutions may be able to reduce interest rate exposure by building an awareness of asset–liability management within parts of the organization involved in such activities and using it to reduce exposure where possible.

Forward Rate Agreements

A forward rate agreement (FRA) is an over-the-counter agreement between two parties, similar to a futures contract, to lock in an interest rate for a short period of time. The period is typically one month or three months, beginning at a future date.

A borrower buys an FRA to protect against rising interest rates, while a lender sells an FRA to protect against declining interest rates. Counterparties to an FRA continue to borrow or invest through normal channels.

TIPS & TECHNIQUES

Interest Rate Basis

When managing interest rate risk, the interest rate, or rate basis, is an important attribute of the risk. Interest rates do not change simultaneously. For example, bank prime rate is an administered rate and can remain unchanged for months while market rates fluctuate significantly.

If hedging products do not match exposure, an organization may not have adequate protection against interest rate risk. Using one interest rate product to hedge another type of exposure may provide an effective hedge at reasonable cost despite there not being a complete match between the hedge and exposure. It is important to understand the implications of matching exposure to a hedging strategy.

In the absence of using derivatives such as basis swaps to restructure exposure, it may be possible to change the basis of an organization's interest rate exposure through its business decisions and activities. For example, a company with prime-based borrowing might negotiate with its lender to use another basis for its interest calculations. An investor may select port-folio assets with returns based on actively traded interest rates.

Rates being hedged should be same or similar to the FRA reference rate to avoid basis risk.

At the beginning of the period covered by the FRA, the reference rate is compared to the FRA rate. If the reference rate is higher, the FRA seller pays a compensating payment (the settlement amount) to the FRA buyer. If the reference rate is lower, the FRA buyer pays the FRA seller. The notional contract amount is used for calculating the settlement amount but is not exchanged.

Although it can occur at the end of the contract term, payment of the settlement amount usually occurs at the beginning of the contract term. In that case, the settlement amount is discounted and the present value of the interest rate differential is paid.

FRAs allow the yield curve to be split into small segments that can be hedged (or traded) independently of one another. A strip of consecutive FRAs can be used to construct a longer-term hedge. For example, a one-year hedge could be constructed using consecutive three-month FRAs.

FRA rates are forward interest rates and are determined by the yield curve. Growth and liquidity in FRAs have been helped tremendously by futures contracts that permit arbitrage and therefore enhance liquidity.

The following information applies to FRAs:

- The forward term of an FRA is the time prior to the beginning of the FRA.

- The contract term is the time covered by the FRA.

- FRA reference rates are posted on major market information services and commonly are LIBOR (London interbank offered rate).

- The settlement amount is the payment to the FRA seller or buyer, based on the differential between the reference rate and the FRA rate at the beginning of the contract period, prorated over the term of the FRA, and usually discounted.

- The maturity of the FRA is the end of the contract term.

Closing Out a Forward Rate Agreement

FRAs can be closed out at current market value. Since both parties have an obligation under an FRA, closing out the contract involves unwinding it through an offsetting transaction. The buyer of an FRA will sell an

Calculating an FRA Settlement Amount

A company needs to borrow $10 million in three months' time. Management is concerned that rates may rise, so the company buys a 3 x 6 FRA at 4.00 percent. The term 3 x 6 indicates that the FRA term begins three months from the trade date and ends six months from the trade date (a term of three months).

If interest rates have risen (as measured by the reference rate compared with the FRA rate), the bank will compensate the company. If the reference rate has fallen, the company will compensate the bank.

FRA rate	4.00%
Reference (actual) rate	5.00%
Difference	1.00%

1.00% x 90 days/360 days[a] x $10 million = $25,000

Since the settlement amount is usually paid at the beginning of the period covered by the FRA, the amount is discounted and its present value paid ($24,691.36) to the company.

[a] The daycount basis in many countries, including the United States, is 360 days. Canada and a few other countries use 365 days.

offsetting FRA, while the seller of an FRA will buy an offsetting FRA, with a resultant gain or loss.

Interest Rate Futures

Interest rate futures are exchange-traded forwards. They permit an organization to manage exposure to interest rates or fixed income prices by locking in a price or rate for a future date. Transacted through a broker, there are commissions to buy or sell and margin requirements.

Unlike FRAs, there is no need to establish a line of credit with a bank. The risk of dealing with other counterparties is replaced with exposure to the exchange clearinghouse.

Interest rate futures may be based on a benchmark interest rate, index, or fixed income instrument. In the case of a bond futures contract, for example, the futures price locks in the price for the bond and thus the resultant yield, since prices and yields move inversely. As with other forwards, locking in a price for the underlying asset, or an

TIPS & TECHNIQUES

Short–Term Interest Rate Futures

Short-term interest rate (STIR) futures trade on several exchanges, including the Chicago Board of Trade, the Chicago Mercantile Exchange, and the Montreal Exchange. These contracts permit hedgers to fix a price for the underlying instrument and therefore the corresponding interest rate, or alternatively the interest rate directly.

IN THE REAL WORLD

Eurodollar Rates

Some sample three-month eurodollar rates, as traded on the Chicago Mercantile Exchange, appear below. The quotes are price indices, from which rates are determined (100 minus price):

December	97.66
March	97.42
June	97.23
September	97.04

interest rate, also means forfeiting the possibility of subsequent favorable market moves.

Eurodollar futures are similar to FRAs for managing interest rate risk and are used in arbitrage with FRAs. These futures contracts are also used for arbitrage in the forward foreign exchange market, enhancing liquidity all around. A Eurodollar futures contract locks in a price for a future delivery and the corresponding interest rate.

Basis risk is a consideration with hedging with futures contracts and other derivatives. Basis risk arises when contracts are used to hedge interest rates other than the contract's underlying rate—for example, exposure to an administered borrowing rate hedged with a Eurodollar contract.

Bond Futures

Bond futures allow investors to hedge existing bond positions, or to replicate bond positions, without buying or selling the underlying bonds. They are useful for tactical asset allocation strategies employed by professional money and portfolio managers. In addition, they can assist in the management of exposure to long-term interest rates.

TIPS & TECHNIQUES

Futures Margin

The futures user must post margin (cash or similar securities) in an account maintained by the broker who facilitated the transaction. Margin is designed to absorb potential subsequent losses on the open futures position. The amount of margin required depends on exchange rules and the nature of the position (e.g., hedging or speculative). Exchange margin requirements are subject to change from time to time, and brokers may require additional margin.

Margin is a performance bond to ensure that the buyer or seller of a futures contract fulfills the obligations associated with the contract. Normally, a futures contract will require initial margin, plus maintenance margin if the futures position suffers loss. Outstanding futures positions are marked-to-market daily, and the margin account of the futures buyer or seller is debited or credited accordingly. By preventing unrealized losses from accumulating, margin helps to safeguard the clearinghouse and the financial system.

Failure to respond to a margin call may lead the broker to close out the futures position by offsetting the contracts outstanding. Costs are the responsibility of the account holder.

Bond futures can be used to hedge bond and interest rate risk, change portfolio asset allocation, or alter portfolio duration.

A borrower can protect against rising rates by selling a bond futures contract provided that the contract underlying interest is similar to the exposure. If interest rates rise (underlying bond price falls), the gain on the futures contract should offset higher market interest rates. If interest rates fall (underlying bond price rises), the loss on the futures contracts should be offset by lower market interest rates. This presumes that there has been no change in the willingness of the organization's lenders to extend credit.

Basis risk can impact the ultimate effectiveness of the hedge. Assuming the futures contract provides a hedge against market interest rates, it will not address other issues such as the deterioration of the hedger's credit quality, which in most cases will differ from the contract's underlying issue.

Bond futures are useful in portfolio management for facilitating tactical and strategic asset allocation. A portfolio manager can alter asset weightings by buying or selling futures contracts without changing actual holdings of securities. The advantages of using bond futures as a proxy to actual purchases of bonds include ease of execution and delivery and potential for reduced transaction costs.

Closing Out a Futures Contract

At expiry, a futures contract can be settled by offsetting it with another futures contract, or by delivering or accepting delivery of the underlying, as permitted. For delivery against bond futures contracts, since deliverable

TIPS & TECHNIQUES

Futures Strips

A strip of futures contracts can also be used to construct a hedge for a longer period of time. The result is similar to an interest rate swap, where consecutive contracts together cover a longer period of time, such as one year. The strategy is limited by the maximum expiry dates of the contracts available.

TIPS & TECHNIQUES

Hedge Ratios

Futures contracts trade in standardized contract amounts and for standardized assets, so a hedge ratio helps to determine the number of contracts needed to ensure an effective hedge. An incorrect number of contracts can mean under- or overhedging. Adjustments are estimates and they are therefore inexact.

Hedge ratios reflect price sensitivities. The goal of hedging is to match a change in the exposure (e.g., bond portfolio) with an offsetting change in the value of a hedge (e.g., futures contract). To determine a hedge ratio, the rate of change of the futures contract is compared with the rate of change of the underlying exposure (although they will be in different directions).

A basic ratio is calculated by dividing nominal exposure by nominal futures contract size. This ratio can be used if the underlying exposure is the same as the futures contract. Otherwise, if the exposure to be hedged differs from the futures contract, the basic ratio can be adjusted. Adjustments may be based on the ratio of basis point values, the correlation between the two interest rates or assets, or another calculation.

For bond futures, the exchange provides a list of bonds that meet delivery requirements. The cheapest-to-deliver bond is the most favorable for the bond seller to deliver, producing the greatest profit or the smallest loss, within delivery requirements. Bond futures prices track the cheapest-to-deliver bond, which itself can change during the futures contract's lifetime. The conversion factor of the cheapest-to-deliver bond, or alternatively duration, may be used to develop a hedge ratio.

TIPS & TECHNIQUES CONTINUED

The hedge ratio may need further adjusting if the exposure differs from the cheapest-to-deliver bond. Historical price data or regression analysis can also be used to develop a hedge ratio. However, relationships between instruments can change and may differ from the historical period tracked. It is for this reason that hedge ratios are an estimate of the number of contracts required.

bonds have different coupons and maturities, a conversion factor is used. Exchanges list deliverable bonds and their conversion factors.

Prior to delivery, a purchased futures contract can be closed out by selling a futures contract with the same delivery date. Similarly, a sold futures contract can be offset by buying a futures contract with the same delivery date.

Commonly, futures contracts are rolled forward to maintain the position. This is accomplished by closing out the near-term delivery contract (buying or selling) and entering into a new contract with farther delivery date (selling or buying).

Interest Rate Swaps

Transacted in the over-the-counter market, interest rate swaps are related to forwards and futures but facilitate interest rate hedging over a longer time interval. Common swaps include asset swaps, basis swaps, zero-coupon swaps, and forward interest rate swaps.

The swap is an agreement between two parties to exchange their respective cash flows. Most commonly, this involves a fixed rate payment exchanged for a floating rate payment. Both parties are obligated by the swap's conditions, and thus there may be a cost to exit from an existing swap, depending on how rates have changed since it was transacted.

Swaps permit a change to the effective nature of an asset or liability without changing the underlying exposure. For example, payment structures can be changed in anticipation of rising interest rates. Alternatively, organizations may be able to take advantage of benefits, such as government or tax incentives, that are available for certain types of financing.

Borrowers with weaker credit ratings may face a credit premium for fixed rate borrowing. Such an organization may borrow at relatively more attractive floating rates and swap for the desired fixed rate payments without any change to the underlying debt. The benefit that accrues can improve the bottom line for both swap parties.

The terms *receiver* and *payer* refer to the fixed rate payment stream in a swap. The benchmark floating rate is, by convention, an average from several market-making financial institutions. Rates are posted on major financial information services. This convention helps avoid con-

TIPS & TECHNIQUES

Swap Counterparties

The principal notional (contractual) amount of an interest rate swap is not exchanged between counterparties but is used to calculate payments. Since only net cash flows are exchanged between counterparties, credit exposure is reduced. However, swaps often have large notional contract amounts and significant terms to maturity, which means the credit quality of counterparties should be monitored. High-quality counterparties should be chosen.

tention over the correct benchmark or opportunities for manipulation. Three-month or six-month LIBOR are common benchmark floating rates. Master agreements are provided by the International Swaps and Derivatives Association (ISDA).

When interest rates are expected to fall, market participants move to floating interest rates, and there is downward pressure on swap spreads. When interest rates are expected to rise, market participants will move to borrow at fixed interest rates, putting upward pressure on swap spreads.

Asset Swaps

A swap to transform an asset's income stream is known as an *asset swap*. Asset swaps allow investors to change the interest rate structure of their revenue streams without changing the structure of the underlying asset. Both interest rate swaps and currency swaps (discussed in Chapter 4) can be asset swaps.

The most popular asset swaps are those that change payments from a fixed interest rate to a floating interest rate, and those that exchange a cash inflow in one currency to another currency.

Asset swaps can also be used to synthetically create a return that would not otherwise be available. For example, consider an investment that offers a floating rate return at a relatively attractive price. An investor that prefers fixed rate assets can buy the floating rate asset and swap the revenue stream for a fixed rate revenue stream without changing the structure of the asset.

Similarly, an investor with foreign currency assets may prefer U.S. dollar revenues that offset a need for U.S. dollars elsewhere in the business. The investor could swap the foreign currency revenues for U.S. dollar revenues without affecting the foreign assets.

IN THE REAL WORLD

Swap Rates

Swap spreads, and therefore all-in swap rates, fluctuate in response to supply and demand. The spread is added to the benchmark (government) yield for the fixed rate, below. A financial institution will pay fixed at the bid rate or receive fixed at the offered rate.

Term of Swap	Governments	Spreads	All-in Rate (bank bid-offer)
2 years	4.40–4.45	20–25	4.60–4.70
3 years	4.60–4.65	25–30	4.85–4.95
4 years	4.70–4.75	25–30	4.95–5.05
5 years	4.95–5.00	25–30	5.20–5.30

A corporate borrower wanting to exchange floating rate payments for fixed rate payments (pay fixed and receive floating) for five years will pay an all-in swap rate of 5.30 (5.00 + .30) percent from the sample swap rates and spreads above.

Basis Swaps

Basis swaps enable counterparties to change exposure from one benchmark floating rate to another. This might permit a better match between an organization's asset and liability cashflows. Basis swaps can also be used to exploit favorable interest rate differentials between indices, or in anticipation of interest rate movements, while maintaining exposure to floating interest rates.

Some rates, such as bank prime rate, are administered and therefore differ from floating or market-determined rates. Administered rates are generally not managed using basis swaps.

Zero-Coupon Swaps

Zero-coupon bonds consist of one payment at maturity comprising principal plus all interest. With no coupon payments, zero-coupon bonds eliminate reinvestment risk for coupon income.

Zero-coupon financing can be desirable but difficult to obtain from a lender, so an alternative is to borrow in another cost-effective way and use a zero-coupon swap to synthetically create the zero-coupon debt. This leaves the original coupon debt unchanged but overlays a zero-coupon structure.

Forward Interest Rate Swaps

Also known as forward-starting interest rate swaps, forward interest rate swaps allow hedgers to arrange a swap in advance of its requirement and commencement. Forward interest rate swaps also allow borrowers and investors to alter cash flows in anticipation of future changes in interest rates or the yield curve.

Additionally, forward interest rate swaps can be used to convert a fixed interest rate to a floating interest rate, or to protect against anticipated rate changes until a fixed rate liability or asset is arranged. At that time, the interest rate swap can be offset with another or can be terminated.

Closing Out an Interest Rate Swap

Interest rate swaps must be settled at market value to be terminated. The market value of a swap at any time after its commencement is the net present value of future cash flows between the counterparties. Swap termination involves the calculation of a settlement amount representing the net present value of all future obligations by each counterparty. This net payment is made to the counterparty with unrealized gains in the swap.

There are several ways to alter or eliminate an existing interest rate swap:

- Offset the swap with another that will produce the required payment streams.

- Cancel the existing swap by paying or receiving a lump sum representing the net present value of remaining payments. This may require a cash payment if the swap has a negative value.

- Extend the swap by blending it with a new one (*blend-and-extend*). This embeds the cost of closing out the swap in the new periodic swap payments.

- Assign the swap to another party that will continue to make and receive payments under the original swap agreement until maturity. The counterparty assigning the swap will either pay to, or receive from, the new counterparty a lump sum that reflects the net present value of all remaining payment streams.

Interest Rate Options

Interest rate options include caps, floors, and collars used to protect against different reference interest rates or prices of underlying assets. Although option strategies usually involve over-the-counter options, they can also be constructed from exchange-traded options.

The business of options is analogous to insurance. One party pays to reduce or eliminate risk, while the other party accepts the risk in exchange for option premium. Option premium paid increases the effective borrowing cost, or decreases the effective return on assets, for hedgers.

Pricing of interest rate options depends on several factors including term to expiry, strike rate, and volatility of the reference interest rate. Prices are normally quoted in basis points of the notional contract amount. The option buyer's specification for contract size, strike rate, reset dates, term to expiry, and reference interest rate can be met with customized options in the over-the-counter market.

Purchased interest rate options can be costly if the underlying rate is volatile. If underlying rates move, but not enough to make the option worth exercising, the option will expire worthless, resulting in a potential loss through adverse market rates as well as the cost of the option premium.

Interest rate options may be cash-settled contracts on interest rates, fixed income instruments such as government bonds, or options on futures contracts. Although the mechanics are similar, the details are important. The hedger should clearly understand the option's underlying interest, permitted delivery opportunities, and the appropriateness of the option as a hedge given the organization's own exposure and objectives.

Basis risk is a consideration in hedging with interest rate options as it is with other interest rate hedges. With options on bond futures, price

TIPS & TECHNIQUES

LIBOR

LIBOR (London Interbank Offered Rate) is the most widely used benchmark or reference rate for short-term interest rates. LIBOR is the interbank rate between major banks for transactions of market size and is calculated from at least eight regular contributor banks. LIBOR is used for settlement of interest rate and futures contracts and lending arrangements. LIBOR rates are posted daily for British pound, Japanese yen, Canadian dollar, Australian dollar, euro, Danish krone, New Zealand dollar, Swiss franc, and U.S. dollar by the British Bankers' Association (BBA) for a range of maturities up to 12 months.

changes may occur as a result of changes in the underlying bond's price, interest rates, or because of a change in the basis. The underlying (cheapest-to-deliver) bond can change during the term of a futures contract, so care should be taken when comparing an option on a futures contract with an option on the bond itself.

Since the buyer has control over its exercise, an option is useful for covering contingent risk, where the anticipated need for a hedge may or may not occur. By avoiding the necessity of locking in an interest rate, even for a short time period, options provide protection against worst-case interest rate scenarios and flexibility for best-case scenarios.

Caps and Floors

Caps and floors are interest rate options packaged to provide protection from changes in interest rates over a period of time. A cap is a series of interest rate options to protect against rising interest rates. A *cap* (sometimes called a *ceiling*) is typically made up of short European-style options, the expiry of each option corresponding to the hedger's anticipated borrowing schedule. In exchange for cap premium, the cap buyer is protected from higher rates (above the cap strike rate) for the period of time covered by the cap.

At the expiry date of each individual option (caplet), the cap seller reimburses the cap buyer if the reference rate is above the cap strike rate. If rates are below the cap rate, the caplet is left to expire, and funding can be obtained at lower market rates. Unexpired portions of the cap (caplets) remain for future borrowing dates.

Compensation to the cap buyer is based on the difference between the strike rate and the reference rate for the notional contract amount and the period of time covered by the option. Although the cost of the cap increases the effective cost of funds for a borrower, it also provides protection and flexibility without locking in a rate.

Interest Rate Cap

A U.S. manufacturer borrows by rolling over short-term debt every quarter. Concerned about rising rates, the company buys an interest rate cap to cover its $10 million floating rate debt. The cap strike rate is 5.00 percent, the reset period is quarterly, and the reference rate is the London Interbank Offered Rate (LIBOR).

- Rollover 1. At the first rollover and cap date, the average reference rate is 4.25 percent. The company will do nothing, since the reference rate is lower than the cap rate. The company will borrow at the lower market rates, and the cap will remain for subsequent rollover dates until its expiry.

- Rollover 2. At the second rollover and cap date, the rate has increased to 5.65 percent. The company will be reimbursed by its bank for the difference between the cap strike rate and the reference rate. Assuming 91 days in the period, this amount is calculated as $10,000,000 x (0.0565 – 0.0500) x 91/ 360 = $16,430.56.

A floor is similar to a cap except that it provides protection against falling rates below the floor strike rate. A floor provides the floor buyer with reimbursement if the reference rate falls below the floor strike rate.

As an alternative to buying a cap, a borrower may sell an interest rate floor, receiving the floor premium. The borrower will be required to pay the floor rate should the floor be exercised by the floor buyer. The floor will be exercised only if interest rates fall. The floor premium received will partially offset higher borrowing costs, but the floor seller still incurs all the risk of rising interest rates and has not hedged against higher rates.

Interest Rate Collar

An interest rate collar comprises a cap and a floor, one purchased and one sold. Collars are often used when caps (or floors) are deemed too expensive. The purchased option provides protection against adverse interest rate movements. The sold option trades away some of the benefits of favorable rates in order to pay for the protective option. Like caps and floors, collars typically consist of a series of interest rate options with expiry dates customized to the hedger's schedule.

If at expiry of each option comprising the collar, the reference rate is between the cap and floor rates, neither the cap nor the floor will be exercised. However, if rates move above the cap rate or below the floor rate, the appropriate option (cap or floor) will be exercised. Effectively, rates will be capped at the cap rate or prevented from falling below the floor rate. If the reference interest rate moves beyond the strike rate, the option is exercised and the option seller pays the option buyer the difference between the reference rate and the strike rate on the notional amount, adjusted for the number of days in that option's term.

Collars may be transacted independently of the underlying exposure they are designed to hedge. In a *zero cost* collar, option premiums offset one another. Like other interest rate options, the collar protects against changing market interest rates but does not provide protection against rate changes as a result of the deterioration of an issuer's credit rating.

Intrinsic value, or the amount that an option is *in-the-money,* is the economic benefit, if any, of exercising the option, as compared with current market prices. Intrinsic value may be positive or zero. Time value is the value attributed to chance that the option may be worthwhile exercising before or at expiry. The greater the time to expiry of an option, the greater the time value and premium, all else being equal. Time value declines more rapidly as expiry approaches. At expiry, time value is zero.

Swaptions

Swaptions are options on interest rate swaps. They give the swaption buyer the right, but not the obligation, to enter into an interest rate swap with predetermined characteristics at or prior to the option's expiry. Swaption premium is paid by the swaption buyer to the swaption seller, typically as a percentage of the notional amount of the swap.

An interest rate swaption can be used to obtain a fixed interest rate (or, alternatively, a floating interest rate). For example, in anticipation of rising interest rates, a swaption buyer can exercise its option to enter into a pay-fixed (receive floating) swap, providing protection against higher rates. The cost of such a strategy is the swaption premium.

The terms *receiver* and *payer* refer to the fixed rate payment stream in a swap:

- The buyer of a payer swaption has the right to enter a pay-fixed (receive floating) swap at the strike rate.

- The buyer of a receiver swaption has the right to enter a receive-fixed (pay floating) swap at the strike rate.

A floating rate borrower can purchase a swaption giving it the right, but not the obligation, to enter into an interest rate swap at the expiry of the swaption. In exchange for this right, the buyer of the swaption pays a premium.

Swaptions may also be sold to earn premium income that can be used to reduce interest costs. The swaption seller takes on potentially unlimited risk because the swaption will only be exercised when the current market is less favorable (to the swaption seller) than the swap strike rate. The swaption seller must be comfortable entering into a swap with the specified terms or, alternatively, not having the swaption exercised.

For the swaption seller, the swaption premium is the only offset for the risk undertaken. The swaption seller may be obligated to enter into the underlying swap, or pay to exit from the obligation, if the swaption is exercisable at expiry. The sale of a swaption alone also does nothing to hedge interest rate exposure.

Exchange-Traded Options

Exchange-traded options may have a futures contract as the underlying interest. Options on interest rates or options on interest rate futures can be used to construct an interest rate cap, floor, or collar. Options may be settled in cash or with the underlying asset or futures contract, depending on exchange rules. Basis risk may be a consideration if exchange-traded options are used for hedging purposes.

When the underlying interest is a futures contract, the purchase of a put option permits the option buyer to sell the futures contract at the strike price, which provides protection against falling (futures) prices. The purchase of a call option on a futures contract allows the option buyer to buy the futures contract at the strike price, providing protection against rising (futures) prices.

Closing Out an Interest Rate Option

In general, if an interest rate option is no longer required and there is time remaining to expiry, it can be sold at market value. For a strategy involving several purchased options, market value is the total of the options that comprise it, and the maximum loss is the cost of the options.

A sold option remains an obligation to the option seller unless it has been closed out by purchasing an offsetting one and the outstanding

TIPS & TECHNIQUES

Interest Rate Futures

Several exchanges offer interest rate contracts:

- Chicago Board of Trade offers futures on 2-, 5-, and 10-year U.S. Treasury notes, Treasury bonds, and 30-day U.S. interest rates.

- Chicago Mercantile Exchange offers bond futures, swap futures, turn futures, and Consumer Price Index (CPI) futures, among other contracts.

- Montreal Exchange offers BA and bond futures and options on futures for Canadian interest rates.

Other international futures exchanges offering interest rate contracts include:

- Euronext-Liffe

- Sydney Futures Exchange

option is canceled. Interest rate collars and other strategies that comprise both purchased and sold options involve such potential obligations.

Sold options with time and/or intrinsic value may be expensive to repurchase. Therefore, the maximum loss may be greater than the original cost (for a package of bought and sold options) or premium received (for sold options).

If not exercised, an option will be worthless if there is no intrinsic value at expiry. Some exchange-traded contracts offer automatic exercise on options that are in-the-money by a certain minimum amount, while others require the option buyer to notify in case of exercise.

At a swaption's expiry, if it is not favorable to use it, the swaption buyer can allow it to expire and transact a swap at market rates. If the swaption is favorable, the swaption buyer can exercise it and enter into the predetermined swap. Alternatively, an in-the-money swaption may be sold, or alternatively closed out with a difference payment from the swaption seller to the swaption buyer.

Summary

- Basic changes to the way that business is conducted may help to minimize an organization's exposure to interest rates.

- Forward rate agreements (FRAs) and futures contracts permit a rate to be fixed for a specific period of time, while swaps permit a hedge to be constructed for a longer period of time.

- A hedge ratio helps to determine the number of exchange-traded contracts needed to ensure an effective hedge. An incorrect number of contracts can result in under- or over-hedging.

- Interest rate caps and floors provide hedgers with protection against rising (or falling) rates, without locking in an interest rate.

CHAPTER 4

Foreign Exchange Risk

 After reading this chapter you will be able to

- Assess ways to reduce foreign exchange exposure through rearranging business processes

- Compare foreign exchange hedging strategies

- Evaluate the risks associated with specific derivatives products and strategies

Although the discussion of hedging usually involves derivatives, it is sometimes possible to minimize currency exposure through prudent modification of business activities. The rearrangement of business processes to reduce risk is a form of internal hedging. It may involve effort but can be a viable means to reduce exposure and risk. Depending on the approach to foreign exchange risk, an organization might undertake internal hedging approaches where available and supplement with derivatives for some or all of the remaining exposure.

Currency Netting

On an organizational or centralized basis, it may be possible to net currency requirements internally. In effect, the organization centralizes some of its banking activities in-house, making excess currency available to other parts of the organization. Market prices, with or without a spread, can be used.

TIPS & TECHNIQUES

Exposure Reduction

A number of techniques have been used to rearrange business activities to reduce foreign exchange exposure, including:

- Currency netting
- Proxy hedging
- Foreign currency debt
- Changes to purchasing/processing
- Transfer exchange rate risk

When an organization has foreign currency cash inflows and outflows, a cash forecast for each currency assists in identifying currency exposures. The forecast format should enable the user to determine a balance for each currency and whether there is a cumulative deficit or excess currency over time based on reasonably certain cashflows. Cumulative gaps between cash inflows and outflows are those that may require hedging. Cashflows that offset over time, for example, over a quarter or a fiscal year, effectively represent a timing issue.

Proxy Hedging

Proxy hedging is a strategy that introduces basis risk intentionally. Groups of currencies, such as those within regional areas, may sometimes exhibit a high correlation to one another. This correlation may be due to similar economic or political prospects or highly regional trade and often involves emerging markets. It is sometimes possible to exploit this correlation for hedging related currencies. If there is strong correlation between the currencies, a proxy currency may be used for hedging purposes in place of one or more currencies.

There are risks inherent in a proxy currency strategy. Although past correlation can be assessed through analysis of historical data, future exchange rate relationships cannot be forecast with accuracy and may be quite different. Domestic factors, such as political instability, can dramatically affect a country's exchange rate in isolation from any regional factors.

As a result, there is no guarantee that historical correlation will have any relation to future correlation. A proxy hedge could result in an organization being unhedged, or under- or overhedged. Obviously, the tradeoff between protection and risk must be weighed carefully and the exposure managed accordingly.

TIPS & TECHNIQUES

Proxy Hedging

There are several reasons why a proxy hedge might be used:

- An organization may find that it is difficult to obtain fair pricing on a particular currency if there is not a highly competitive market for the currency or the market is controlled.

- An organization might have exposure to several related currencies, each of which is too small for an effective hedging program.

- There might be significant regional effects on individual currencies.

- Currency hedging products for the particular currency of exposure may not be available.

Foreign Currency Debt

The issuance of foreign currency debt is sometimes used to reduce foreign exchange exposure. There are several reasons for borrowing in a foreign currency. Issuers may want to entice specific institutional investors by issuing in a desirable currency. Lower foreign interest rates might be seen as a way to reduce funding costs. Foreign currency debt may be required to finance an overseas expansion or investment in foreign plant and operations.

The exchange rate risk in foreign currency debt cannot typically be hedged using a forward without eliminating the interest rate savings, because forward rates are derived from interest rates. The forward rate is

IN THE REAL WORLD

Foreign Currency Debt

The translated value of unhedged foreign currency debt, regardless of the attractiveness of the interest rate, can quickly increase if exchange rates move adversely. The effect of exchange rate changes on foreign currency debt can be seen in the following table, which shows the translated value of a 10 million liability in British pound sterling (GBP) to a U.S. organization under several exchange rate scenarios:

Exchange Rate (USD per GBP)	Translated Liability in U.S. Dollars
1.4300 USD/GBP	USD 14,300,000
1.6300 USD/GBP	USD 16,300,000
1.8300 USD/GBP	USD 18,300,000
2.0300 USD/GBP	USD 20,300,000

based on the interest rate differential between the two currencies before taking into account credit spreads.

The risk of debt denominated in a foreign currency can be reduced when the borrower has an offsetting asset denominated in the same currency, such as an income-producing subsidiary. If income from the asset is adequate to offset the payments on the liability, and it can be expected to continue for the life of the debt, the organization can take advantage of it. This may provide lower foreign currency borrowing rates while reducing the exchange rate risk already inherent in foreign currency receivables. If the foreign currency strengthens and the market value of the debt increases, the value of the offsetting foreign currency revenues should also increase.

However, offsetting foreign currency debt with foreign currency revenues does not take into account how demand and revenues change in response to exchange rates. Foreign currency revenues may be sensitive to exchange rates. If changes in exchange rates impact revenues and the ability to service foreign-currency-denominated debt, this must be taken into account.

Changes to Purchasing/Processing

Managing foreign exchange transaction risk can sometimes be accomplished through offsetting transactions to reduce currency exposure. This might involve different sources or locations for manufacturing. A company with foreign currency sales might use a supplier whose products are priced in the same currency.

Longer-term strategies might involve manufacturing in key customer locations or obtaining new customers where inputs are sourced. Exploiting exchange rate differences is often a reason to relocate manufacturing or sourcing, although there are other ramifications. A number of regions have experienced growth in manufacturing as a result of exchange rate differences.

TIPS & TECHNIQUES

Project Bids

Bids on foreign projects often require a foreign exchange rate component to be embedded in the price of the contract. There is a risk that rates may change dramatically once the bid has been submitted but before notification to the winning bidder occurs. Some companies manage this risk by inserting a currency adjustment clause into the contract. If the exchange rate moves more than a predetermined amount, the contract price must be adjusted to reflect the exchange rate change. This shifts the exchange rate risk to the purchaser. Compound options, discussed later in this chapter, are also used for bid situations.

Transfer Exchange Rate Risk

It is sometimes possible to transfer exchange rate risk to customers or suppliers. For example, changes may be made to pricing methodology to better reflect exchange rates. In some industries, surcharges help to offset exchange rate risk and pass it on to the final customer. Alternatively, it might be possible to obtain fixed prices in two currencies from suppliers and pay the lower price when invoiced.

Other strategies include offering customers the opportunity to pay in another currency, which might help them offset their own currency exposure. Permanent migration of pricing transactions in currencies that are widely traded, such as U.S. dollars or euros, may be attractive to customers and reduce currency exposure. Prices should be offered in one currency, rather than a choice of currencies, since the latter increases uncertainty and exposure.

TIPS & TECHNIQUES

Combined Commodity
and Currency Exposure

Commodity prices often involve exchange rates, since many commodities trade in world markets in major currencies such as U.S. dollars. Some opportunities for managing combined commodity and currency exposure include:

- Where possible, request that commodities be priced in their normal currency of trade (e.g., U.S. dollars). A supplier might offer fixed prices in dual currencies, which provides flexibility and inherent value.

- Track and forecast net commodity exposure in the currency in which it trades.

- Track and forecast currency exposure that arises as a result of commodity-related transactions.

- Provide conservative currency and commodity rates for internal pricing and sales purposes.

- Ensure prices used for external purposes are kept current.

- Offer prices in major currencies. For example, non-U.S. customers may prefer prices in U.S. dollars to offset their other U.S. dollar exposures. This should be provided as a one-time choice, rather than on an ongoing basis.

- Avoid offering dual currency pricing to customers because it shifts currency risk back to the organization.

Fixed-price contracts are an alternative way to effectively shift foreign exchange risk to a supplier. However, if the supplier does a poor job of managing the risk, product prices may be expected to rise and slow to subsequently fall. At best, fixed-price contracts provide a lag time before exchange rate changes affect pricing.

Forward Contracts

Forward foreign exchange markets facilitate the movement of capital between domestic and international money markets and the hedging of foreign exchange risk. Hedging foreign exchange exposure with derivatives such as forward contracts replaces exposure to exchange rates with exposure to the performance of contractual counterparties. Therefore, it is important to understand credit risk, which is discussed in Chapter 5.

A foreign exchange forward is a customized contract that locks in an exchange rate for the purchase or sale of a predetermined amount of currency at a future delivery date. Since foreign exchange always involves two currencies, a contract to buy one currency is a contract to sell the other currency. Most contracts are outright forwards that lock in an exchange rate for a specific forward delivery date, but there are variations.

By locking in an exchange rate, the organization has eliminated the potential for adverse currency movements, but it has also given up the potential for favorable movements. Whether the currency moves adversely or favorably, the forward contract provides exchange rate certainty for the amount hedged and obligates the parties to it.

An organization with foreign currency accounts receivable can sell its expected excess currency forward. Similarly, an organization with foreign currency accounts payable can buy its currency requirements forward.

Forwards typically have maturity dates as far as one to two years forward, although if credit concerns are not an issue they may be more

Foreign Exchange Forward

A company requires 100 million Japanese yen in three months to pay for imported products. The current spot exchange rate is 115.00 yen per U.S. dollar, and the forward rate is 114.50. The company books a forward contract to buy yen (sell U.S. dollars) in three months' time at a price of 114.50 and orders its merchandise.

In three months' time, the company will use the contract to buy yen at 114.50. At that time, if yen is trading at 117.00 per U.S. dollar, the company will have locked in a price that, with the benefit of hindsight, is worse than current market prices. If three months later yen is at 112.00 per U.S. dollar, the company will have successfully protected itself against a more expensive yen.

Regardless of price changes, the company has locked in its yen purchase price at the forward rate of 114.50, enabling it to budget its costs with certainty. Presuming that exchange rate certainty was the goal of the forward contract, it will have achieved that goal.

long-dated. Forwards trade in the over-the-counter market, and the forward price includes a profit for the dealer. The forward market for major currencies is very liquid, due in part to the fact that forwards can be replicated in the interest rate markets.

Credit facilities with a financial institution are required to transact forwards. This may be a separate credit facility specifically for foreign exchange, and it should be arranged in advance of the time that the forward is required.

Forward Rates

The forward price is based on the spot exchange rate, plus or minus a forward spread (forward points). Sample spot and forward prices (Canadian dollars per U.S. dollar) for several delivery dates follow:

Delivery	Forward Points	All-in Rate
Spot	–	1.2895
1 month	+20	1.2915
2 months	+35	1.2930
3 months	+50	1.2945
6 months	+90	1.2985
1 year	+160	1.3055
2 years	+240	1.3135

Forward Pricing

The forward price reflects the difference in interest rates between the two currencies over the period of time covered by the forward. The interest rate differential may be positive or negative, resulting in a forward price that is at a premium or discount to the spot rate.

A change in either the spot rate or the underlying interest rates will change the forward price. The spot price, plus or minus the forward points, equals the forward price or *all-in* price.

Flexible Forwards

A variation on a standard forward contract is an option-dated or flexible forward. These contracts permit the forward to be used on a date of the hedger's choice within an allowable date range. Some contracts permit up to three separate delivery dates, providing additional flexibility.

Flexible forwards can be useful for organizations that find it difficult to forecast a specific date for a forward. However, they are necessarily priced to the least favorable date from the customer's standpoint, so the flexibility involves a cost.

Nondeliverable Forwards

Nondeliverable forwards are contractual agreements where delivery of the currency does not occur. Similar to a cash-settled futures contract, at the forward date, the current spot rate is compared to the contracted forward rate and a cash payment changes hands. Nondeliverable forwards are often used for hedging emerging market currencies where delivery is difficult.

Closing Out a Forward Contract

Once a forward contract has been transacted, the exchange rate is fixed for the amount and delivery date. To take delivery under the terms of

TIPS & TECHNIQUES

Foreign Exchange Points

Most currencies are quoted to four decimal places. The Japanese yen is a notable exception, quoted to two decimal places in the indirect (yen per U.S. dollars) method. A foreign exchange point is an increment or decrement of one at the last standard decimal place. For example, a point is the difference between 1.3501 and 1.3502 (Canadian dollars per U.S. dollar), or the difference between 120.11 and 120.12 (Japanese yen per U.S. dollar).

the forward at maturity, the organization should provide instructions to the financial institution at least one or two days prior to maturity.

A forward contract can be closed out in one of several ways:

- Undertake delivery according to the terms of the forward contract.

- Close out the forward contract by buying or selling an offsetting contract at prevailing market rates, with a resultant gain or loss.

- Extend or roll the contract forward to another date at current rates.

Swaps

Swaps trade in the over-the-counter market between large financial institutions and their customers. Although they are similar, there are some significant differences between foreign exchange and currency swaps. Foreign exchange swaps tend to have shorter terms to maturity and have only two exchanges between counterparties. Currency swaps tend to cover longer periods and involve multiple exchanges between counterparties.

Foreign Exchange Swaps

Foreign exchange swaps are used extensively, particularly by financial institutions, to manage cash balances and exposures in various currencies. Traders also use swaps to facilitate the trading of forwards or the interest rate differential between two currencies.

A foreign exchange swap consists of a spot transaction and forward transaction. One currency is bought at the spot date, with a reversing sale at the forward date. Both the spot price and the forward price are set when the trade is made, and the difference (the forward points) is the net cost of, or gain resulting from, the swap.

For nonfinancial institutions, foreign exchange swaps are often used to facilitate short-term investing or borrowing in nondomestic currencies. They effectively create an investment in one currency and a loan in another. Foreign exchange swaps terms are typically about a year or less.

Currency Swaps

Currency swaps enable swap counterparties to exchange payments in different currencies, changing the effective nature of an asset or liability without altering the underlying exposure. Currency swaps usually have periodic payments between the counterparties for the term of the swap and cover a longer period of time than foreign exchange swaps.

A currency swap might be useful for a company that has issued long-term foreign currency debt to finance capital expenditures. If the company prefers to make debt payments in its domestic currency, it can enter into a currency swap to effectively exchange its required foreign currency payments for domestic currency payments. Currency swaps can also be used to lock in the cost of existing foreign currency debt or change the revenue stream on an asset.

A currency swap is similar to a loan combined with an investment. An exchange takes place at the beginning of the currency swap. Over the term of the swap, each party makes regular periodic payments in the desired currency and receives periodic payments in the other currency. As a result, currency swap payments are not usually netted. At the swap's maturity, there is an exchange back to the original currencies.

Currency swaps come in three basic forms. The classic currency swap involves a change in the currency. A currency basis (floating-to-floating) swap involves a change in the currency and the type of floating interest rate (the basis). Alternatively, and most commonly, a cur-

Currency Swaps

Currency swaps permit companies to borrow in markets where they have the greatest advantage and then swap to effectively obtain the desired currency of payment. The following are reasons companies may have an advantage borrowing in a foreign currency:

- A well-known issuer name

- Foreign investor demand for assets in the currency

- Regulatory or tax advantages

- Local government programs that favor a particular type of debt

- Subsidies of various kinds

rency swap involves both a change in the currency and a change from floating to fixed (or vice versa).

Closing Out a Swap

Currency swaps are relatively liquid instruments that can be assigned, terminated, or overlaid with another swap. A currency swap can be closed out by settling the net present value of remaining payments between the counterparties. Existing swaps can also be blended with new swaps or extended, where the cost of closing out the swap is embedded into the new agreement.

Foreign exchange swaps can be closed out by settling with an offsetting swap, resulting in a gain or a loss depending on forward prices at the time of closing out the swap.

Currency Futures

Currency futures are exchange-traded forward contracts to buy or sell a predetermined amount of currency on a future delivery date. Contract size, expiry dates, and trading are standardized by the exchange on which they trade.

Several exchanges offer currency futures, including the following:

- International Monetary Market (IMM) division of the Chicago Mercantile Exchange

- New York Board of Trade

- Philadelphia Stock Exchange

The futures contract allows a currency buyer or seller to lock in an exchange rate for future delivery, removing the uncertainty of exchange rate fluctuations prior to the contract's expiry. Unlike forward contracts, there is no need for a foreign exchange line of credit with a financial institution because contracts are transacted through a broker or futures commission merchant. Both commissions and margin requirements apply.

TIPS & TECHNIQUES

Reporting Limits

Reporting limits are used by exchanges as part of their market intelligence operations. Reporting limits help exchanges prevent the kind of aggressive market manipulation that hampers legitimate hedging and trading. Member firms of the exchange are required to report individuals or firms whose futures positions exceed exchange reporting limits.

Currency futures prices are normally quoted in the inverted or direct method. U.S. futures exchanges quote rates as U.S. dollars per foreign currency unit. This is in contrast to the over-the-counter market where most currencies are normally quoted in the indirect method as foreign currency units per U.S. dollar.

Performance of parties to a futures contract is guaranteed by a clearing corporation, replacing exposure to any individual contract holder. Exposure to the clearing corporation still exists.

Mark-to-Market and Margin

Futures contracts involve contractual obligations between a buyer and seller and permit control of a larger position in the underlying currency. Margin is a performance bond, required by both buyers and sellers, to ensure their performance to the contract. Exchanges determine minimum initial and maintenance margin, and exchange members (brokers) may require additional margin, depending on the contract and type of position.

Margin cash is deposited with the broker that facilitated the transaction. Futures contracts are repriced or marked-to-market daily, and each margin account is debited or credited with the day's losses or gains. When the market value of a futures position declines and losses are incurred, additional margin may be required to maintain the position. Failure to respond to a margin call will result in the position being closed out at the cost of the account holder.

Closing Out a Futures Contract

A futures contract can be closed out in one of several ways:

- Take delivery of the currency per the terms of contract.
- Close out the contract by buying (or selling) an offsetting contract at prevailing market rates, with a resultant gain or loss.

- Extend or roll the contract forward to another delivery date.

A long futures contract is closed out by selling a futures contract with the same delivery date. A sold futures contract can be offset by buying a futures contract with the same expiry date. Exchange rules determine the latest date at which an outstanding contract can be closed out.

The majority of futures contracts do not involve delivery. Most are closed out or rolled forward prior to expiry. Rolling forward involves closing out existing contract and entering into a new contract with another delivery date.

Foreign Exchange Options

Foreign exchange options can be a useful adjunct to a foreign exchange hedging program. The purchase of options can reduce the risk of an adverse currency movement, while maintaining the ability to profit from favorable exchange rate changes. The sale of options can be used to produce option premium income, though not providing a hedge.

Foreign exchange options are similar to insurance. The option buyer pays an option premium for protection from adverse exchange rate changes, while the option seller accepts the risk in exchange for receiving option premium. The contract permits the notional amount of a currency to be bought or sold at the strike rate, until or at the expiry date.

Most foreign exchange options trade in the over-the-counter market. However, they also trade in the exchange-traded market at the Chicago Mercantile Exchange, the Philadelphia Stock Exchange, and the New York Board of Trade. For exchange-traded options, contracts are accessed through a broker, and commissions and margin requirements apply.

A put option gives the option buyer the right to sell the underlying currency at the strike rate. If the option buyer exercises the put, the option seller has the obligation to accept the currency at the strike rate.

A call option gives its buyer the right to purchase the underlying currency at the strike rate. If the option buyer exercises the call, the option seller has the obligation to deliver the currency at the strike rate.

Since foreign exchange options always involve currency pairs, a call on one currency is necessarily a put on the other currency. For example, an option that permits the purchase of Swiss francs against Japanese yen is a call option on francs and a put option on yen.

Exotic options are over-the-counter options with special attributes. *Path dependent options,* such as average rate options, have a payoff that depends on the activity of the underlying currency before the option's expiry. *Barrier options,* such as knock-in and knock-out options, are dependent on the achievement of a predetermined exchange rate barrier prior to expiry.

Fundamentals

Options normally possess one of two standard exercise features, although others do exist. An American-style option is exercisable at any time before expiry of the option. A European-style option is exercisable on the expiry date. All else being equal, European-style options cost less than American-style options because there is less opportunity for them to be exercised.

Options are available in major currencies, and generally in any currency with an actively traded spot and forward market. Over-the-counter option contracts are customized with respect to strike price, contract size, and expiry date.

Exchange-traded currency options have standardized expiry dates, contract amounts, and strike prices. There are also a few customizable products. The underlying interest may be the currency itself or a currency futures contract.

The relationship between the strike rate and current exchange rate helps to determine option premium and how much the option's value will respond to exchange rate changes. An at-the-money option permits the option holder to exercise it at a rate equivalent to current market rates (usually the forward rate). An in-the-money option has a strike rate that is more favorable exchange than current rates. An out-of-the-money option has a strike rate that is worse than current exchange rates. The out-of-the-money option's value is based on the probability of it being in-the-money before expiry.

TIPS & TECHNIQUES

Delta Hedging

An option's delta is the rate of change of the option's value given a change in the underlying exchange rate. It is a measure of the option's sensitivity to movements in the exchange rate and is based on the probability that the option will be worth exercising before it expires. An option's value depends on the relationship of the strike price to the market exchange rate, in addition to other factors that affect the option's price.

Delta hedging involves rebalancing a position in the underlying currency to hedge the option exposure. Delta hedging is one of the ways that options traders hedge their option positions. When the underlying currency moves by more than a small amount, the option's delta changes and the hedge must be adjusted. Gamma measures the rate of change of delta.

An option's strike price is important from a hedging perspective. When an option is purchased as a hedge, it is possible the exchange rate will move adversely but not enough to make the option worth exercising. If the option is out-of-the-money at expiry, it will expire worthless, resulting in a loss on the underlying exposure and the amount of option premium paid.

Volatility measures the market's perception of the variability of the exchange rate. Option traders often speculate on volatility as a component of the underlying currency. Volatility is an important component of an option's price, and an increase in volatility increases option premiums, all else being equal. The result is that options are most expensive when their protection is most desirable. As volatility rises, the option

TIPS & TECHNIQUES

Foreign Exchange
Option Prices

Foreign exchange option prices, or premiums, are based on:

- Current exchange rate

- Exercise or strike rate

- Risk-free foreign interest rate

- Risk-free domestic interest rate

- Volatility of the exchange rate

- Whether the option is a put or a call

- Time until expiration of the option

- Exercise privileges (e.g., American-style or European-style)

TIPS & TECHNIQUES

Intrinsic Value
and Time Value

Option premiums consist of intrinsic value plus time value. Intrinsic value is the amount an option is in-the-money, if any. Time value is the market's measure of the probability of an option becoming in-the-money if it is not already. An option's time value does not change in a linear fashion with the passage of time but erodes more rapidly as expiry approaches. Presuming the option is not yet in-the-money, the chances of it being exercisable become smaller as expiry approaches, and this is reflected by the option's diminishing time value.

seller's risk increases, offsetting the higher premium received. Although historical volatility is tracked and monitored, traders use implied volatility in pricing decisions, which is the level of volatility implied by options prices.

Buying Options

An option buyer achieves protection against adverse exchange rates beyond the strike rate for a specified currency amount and expiry date. The option buyer maintains the flexibility to take advantage of favorable exchange rates should they materialize. For this benefit, the option buyer pays option premium to the option seller.

At the option's expiry, if the option is in-the-money, the option holder can exercise it or sell it. The exercise privilege rests with the option buyer. If an organization wishes to exercise a purchased option, it must inform the financial institution or broker that it wishes to do so by providing instructions. Although some exchange-traded options offer automatic exercise if certain conditions are met, the responsibility to exercise an in-the-money option rests with the option buyer.

The maximum loss with the purchase of a currency option is the premium paid for it, while the organization can participate in subsequent favorable exchange rate movements. From a hedging perspective, the option premium is the cost of hedging.

EXAMPLE

Purchase of Currency Option

A U.S. company sells medical equipment to Canada and wants to protect its exposure to a decline in the value of its Canadian dollar receivables. The company has been budgeting an exchange rate of U.S.$0.7500, but the Canadian dollar is projected to weaken. The company expects to receive about C$10 million in about six months.

The company buys a Canadian dollar put option (U.S. dollar call) that provides the right, but not the obligation, to sell Canadian dollars at U.S.$0.7500 strike price. The option premium of $200,000 reduces the company's effective selling rate for its Canadian dollars.

- *Scenario 1.* Six months later, the Canadian dollar has strengthened to U.S.$0.8000. The company lets the option expire and sells Canadian dollars in the market at U.S.$0.8000.

- *Scenario 2.* Six months later, the Canadian dollar has weakened to U.S.$0.7000. The company exercises its option and sells Canadian dollars at the strike price of U.S.$0.7500.

Selling Options

In general, the sale of options entails significantly more risk than the purchase of options. The seller receives option premium and is obligated to the terms of the option. Since exchange rates can move dramatically, a worst-case scenario may not be quantifiable in advance.

Selling an option does not provide a hedge against currency exposure, although the premium received provides some cushion against adverse exchange rates. The risk of an adverse currency fluctuation must be managed and the option seller may have to take additional measures if the currency begins to move adversely.

The premium received depends on factors including volatility and time value. The more volatile the currency, the greater the chance for it to be exercised and the more premium it will generate, all else being equal.

An organization with foreign currency sales could sell a call option and receive option premium. If the currency subsequently rallies, the call option will be exercised against the option seller and the option seller will be obligated to sell the underlying currency at the strike rate. This may be unattractive compared with current exchange rates. Alternatively, if the underlying currency declines (the exposure of greatest concern

IN THE REAL WORLD

Notable Quote

"The financial markets have some complicated features, but good common sense goes a lot further than mathematical flash and dash."

Source: Charles W. Smithson, respected risk management author, educator, and executive, in *Managing Financial Risk,* copyright Richard D. Irwin Inc., 1995.

to the organization), the call option will not be exercised and the hedger will need to take other steps to protect against losses.

Although the maximum gain from the sale of an option is the option premium, the maximum loss cannot be determined in advance. The maximum loss from the sale of an unhedged call is theoretically unlimited, since the option seller does not obtain any protection as a result of the sold option beyond option premium received. The maximum loss from the sale of an unhedged put is potentially very large,

---

EXAMPLE

Foreign Exchange Collar

A company needs protection against a rising U.S. dollar (declining Canadian dollar) one month from now. The current exchange rate is 1.2500 CAD/USD. The company enters into a zero-cost collar with its bank by purchasing a call option with a strike price of 1.2700 CAD/USD and selling a put option with a strike price of 1.2300 CAD/USD. Both options are European-style with the same one-month expiry dates.

There are three potential scenarios. If the exchange rate moves above 1.2700 CAD/USD, the company will exercise the call option and buy U.S. dollars at 1.2700. The sold put option will expire worthless. Alternatively, if the exchange rate moves below 1.2300, the bank will exercise the sold put option and the company will be required to buy U.S. dollars from the bank at 1.2300. The company's call option will expire worthless. If the exchange rate remains between 1.2300 and 1.2700, neither option will be exercised, both will expire worthless, and the company's U.S. dollar requirements will be purchased at current market rates.

---

although the currency can only fall to zero. As a result, the sale of options has a much higher risk profile than the purchase of options.

Foreign Exchange Collar

Options can be costly if the exchange rate is volatile. To reduce the cost of hedging, *collars* are often used. Various names have been applied to a collar, including range forward, cylinder option, tunnel option, and zero-cost collar. A collar combines the purchase of a call option and the sale of a put option with the same expiry date on the same currency pair.

European-style options are normally used to ensure that only one of the two options is exercised. The sold option generates option premium to pay for the purchased option. Strike prices are often chosen so that the premium of the sold option offsets the premium of the purchased option and the collar has a zero cost. Since only one option will be exercised, collars limit the effective exchange rate, the upper exchange rate by the call, and the lower exchange rate by the put.

Average Rate Options

Average rate or Asian options have a payoff that depends on the average exchange rate over the option's term to expiry. They allow an organization to hedge an exchange rate for a number of currency transactions over a period of time such as one year. At expiry of the option, the average rate is calculated from the periodic fixings made during the term and compared with the strike price.

There are several different variants, including fixed strike and floating strike rate types. For a fixed strike average rate option, if the average rate is worse than the strike rate, the option buyer is compensated for the difference between the average rate and the strike rate.

Average rate options are often used where foreign exchange transactions occur on an ongoing and regular basis. Depending on the type

TIPS & TECHNIQUES

Pegged Exchange Rates

Pegged exchange rates, where a currency's exchange rate is pegged to another currency or a basket of currencies, appear to provide a simple solution to exchange rate risk. The foreign central bank manages the exchange rate and prevents it from moving beyond the target peg rate or range. From a hedging perspective, however, pegged exchange rates should be approached with caution. A significant market move or even a currency crisis may result if there is aggressive selling of the currency and the foreign central bank cannot defend the pegged rate. What previously appeared to be a low-volatility currency can quickly become a high-volatility currency.

of average rate option, they may provide a lower cost hedge than other options, which makes them attractive to hedgers.

Barrier Options

The payoff for a barrier option is contingent on the exchange rate reaching the barrier level. Once reached, the option may become exercisable (knock-in option) or become unexercisable (knock-out option). Knock-in options may be "up-and-in" or "down-and-in," while knock-out options may "up-and-out" or "down-and-out," depending on the terms of the contract. Knock-in options normally become conventional European-style options if the knock-in rate is reached. Barrier options have both a strike rate and a barrier (knock-in or knock-out) rate.

The buyer of a knock-out option pays option premium for a European-style option that exists unless the exchange rate passes a predetermined level, at which point the option knocks out and becomes unexercisable. The knock-out level is chosen by the option buyer and may be a rate at which a hedge is no longer required. If a knock-out option becomes unexercisable and has to be replaced because a hedge is still needed, this will increase the cost of hedging.

Both knock-out options and knock-in options are popular due to their cost and simplicity. Since there is no guarantee that the option will be exercisable, there is less risk to the option seller, and they normally cost less than a conventional option as a result. Protection is provided

IN THE REAL WORLD

Knock-Out Option

An importer is concerned that British pound sterling will increase against the U.S. dollar, reducing the company's profit margins. The treasurer buys a knock-out call option on sterling with a strike price of $1.8500. The knock-out rate is set at 1.8100, at which rate the treasurer would be more comfortable locking it in with a forward. The option premium paid for the option effectively increases sterling's cost under all scenarios:

- If sterling increases, the option can be exercised at $1.8500 if needed.

- If sterling decreases, the option may get knocked out, but rates will be more attractive.

- The worst-case scenario is that the option gets knocked out and sterling subsequently rises, leaving the company without rate protection. The company should consider another hedge if the option gets knocked out and protection is still required.

against unfavorable exchange rates, while allowing full participation in any favorable movements.

The closer the knock-out level is to the current market price, the less premium will need to be paid for the option. Clearly, the closer the knock-out level to the market price, the more likely it is that the option will be knocked out and not be exercisable. The reverse is true for a knock-in option.

However, if the exchange rate does not reach the barrier level (in the case of a knock-in) or is knocked out (in the case of a knock-out), the hedger has no option, and therefore no protection against exchange rates. Therefore, a strike price should be chosen carefully.

Compound Options

Compound options are options on options. Normally European-style, they give the option buyer the right, but not the obligation, to buy or sell an option contract at the compound option's expiry date at a pre-determined option premium. Although they are initially cheaper than standard options, if both the compound option and its underlying

TIPS & TECHNIQUES

Compound Options

Compound options are often used to protect against the currency exposure inherent in major bids, where there may be a significant time lag between pricing and the announcement of the successful bid winner. In exchange for option premium, the organization can protect a worst-case option premium cost for the option that might be required if the contract is won.

option are purchased, the total hedging cost may be greater than with an ordinary put or call option.

Closing Out an Option

If not exercised, a purchased option may be allowed to expire, at which time it will be worthless if it is not in-the-money. The decision to exercise the option rests with the option buyer. A sold option remains a potential obligation to the option seller until it has been purchased back and the obligation canceled.

An option contract can be closed out in one of several ways:

- Take/make delivery per terms of option contract at discretion of option holder.

- Sell a purchased option at current market value.

- Buy back a sold option at current market value.

- Allow the option to expire at discretion of option holder.

Closing out a foreign exchange collar—which involves both purchased and sold options—requires buying back the sold options and selling the purchased options. There may be a cost to exit from the collar if the sold options are worth more than the purchased options. Therefore, the cost to close out the collar may be greater than its original cost.

Summary

- Foreign exchange hedging using derivatives replaces exposure to foreign exchange rates with exposure to foreign exchange counterparties.

- There are a number of ways to reduce exchange rate exposure that do not involve the use of derivatives. However, they typically involve renegotiating or changing process and as a result, they may take time and organizational resources to implement.

- Forwards and futures lock in an exchange rate for a particular delivery date. Option buyers obtain protection from adverse exchange rate changes, while option sellers accept risk in exchange for receipt of option premium.

CHAPTER 5

Credit Risk

After reading this chapter you will be able to

- Describe the major sources of credit and counterparty risk
- Identify common methods for managing credit risk
- Explain the basic types of credit derivatives

Credit risk is a factor in every business. It exists whenever payment or performance to a contractual agreement by another organization is expected, and it is the likelihood of a loss arising from default or failure of another organization.

Credit risk and the methods used to manage it depend to a certain extent on the size and complexity of exposures. Financial institutions, such as banks, investment dealers, trust companies, insurance companies, and credit unions, typically have significant credit exposure due to their emphasis on lending and trading. Although credit risk is traditionally associated with lending, it is also a major and often overlooked concern for other business entities such as corporations.

How Credit Risk Arises

Conventional credit risk arises through lending, investing, and credit granting activities and concerns the return of borrowed money or the payment for goods sold. Credit risk also arises through the performance of counterparties in contractual agreements such as derivatives. When a financial obligation is not fully discharged, either because the counterparty cannot or will not fulfill its obligations, a loss may result.

Poor economic conditions and high interest rates contribute to the likelihood of default for many organizations. Credit or counterparty failure is also more likely when an organization has accumulated large losses, owes many other counterparties, or when an organization's creditors or counterparties have financial difficulty or have failed.

Credit risk is often considered a one-way risk, because it exists when an organization is owed payment or an obligation by another party.

Credit risks include:

- Default risk

- Counterparty pre-settlement risk

- Counterparty settlement risk

- Legal risk

- Sovereign or country risk

- Concentration risk

Default Risk

Traditional credit risk involves the default on a payment, typically related to lending or sales. For example, a debt issuer is said to be in default when it indicates it will not make a contractual interest payment to lenders. The likelihood of the default occurring is known as the probability of default.

Depending on the nature of the lending agreement, the amount at risk from a default may be as much as the entire liability. Amounts may later be recovered that reduce the size of the loss. The likelihood of a recovery depends on several factors, including the creditor's legal status. However, if an organization fails because of large outstanding obligations or losses, which is usually the case, later collections may be difficult or impossible.

Counterparty Pre-Settlement Risk

A major source of credit risk in financial markets arises from exposure to counterparties in financial derivatives such as swaps, forwards, and options. These credit risks are referred to as counterparty risks since they arise from transactions with counterparties. The credit risk that results from such transactions includes pre-settlement risk and settlement risk, both types of default.

Pre-settlement risk or replacement risk arises from the possibility of counterparty default once a contract has been entered into but prior to settlement. In the event of a default, it might be necessary to enter into a replacement contract at far less favorable prices. The risk associated with the pre-settlement period is that a contract has unrealized gains, for example, in offsetting an exposure, and that the counterparty's failure will result in the loss of that benefit to the organization.

Should a counterparty fail to fulfill its obligation, the potential impact to an organization depends on how market rates have changed since the original contract was established. From a risk management perspective, the loss of a contract with no market value—or negative market value, as might be the case with an interest rate swap that has unrealized losses—is of much less concern than one with unrealized gains. However, note that bankruptcy laws and rules, which vary from region to region, play a role in the eventual outcome of such a default.

Losses from the failure of a counterparty can also be evaluated in terms of current and potential exposure to an organization. Current exposure is the organization's exposure if the counterparty defaulted on its obligation at current market rates. Potential exposure is an estimate of losses if a counterparty were to default under different rate scenarios.

Counterparty Settlement Risk

Settlement risk is a transaction risk arising from the exchange of payments between parties to an agreement. Settlement risk is the risk that payment is made but not received, and it may result in large losses because the entire payment is potentially at risk during the settlement process. The size of the loss depends on the size of the payments, whether both parties make payments, how payments are made, and whether any residual amount can be collected after a payment failure.

Settlement risk is often associated with foreign exchange trading, where payments in different money centers are not made simultaneously and volumes are huge. Counterparties traditionally pay one another in different currencies, with most transactions settling one or two days after the trade date. There is usually a time delay between an organization initiating an outbound settlement payment and the confirmation of the arrival of an inbound payment from the organization's trade counterparty.

Settlement risk is currently being addressed with strategic global initiatives including continuous linked settlement (CLS), netting, and

IN THE REAL WORLD

Herstatt Risk

Settlement risk is sometimes referred to as *Herstatt risk*. Bankhaus Herstatt was a small German bank that was active in foreign exchange before it failed in 1974. On the day German regulators shut it down, it had received payments from foreign exchange counterparties but had yet to make its own payments to others. Counterparty financial institutions in New York and elsewhere suffered losses as a result.

payment with finality. CLS, in particular, has had a significant impact on settlement risk in foreign exchange trading. These global initiatives are discussed in more detail in Chapter 10.

An additional source of settlement risk arises through the payment systems of various countries and the financial institutions that participate in them. Daylight overdraft limits may permit financial institutions to be overdrawn intra-day, thus increasing risk for the central bank, which in many cases acts as a guarantor.

Legal Risk

Legal risk is the risk that an organization is not legally permitted or able to enter into transactions, particularly derivatives transactions. The risk extends to the individuals who make decisions on behalf of counterparties and their level of authorization to enter into transactions.

It is necessary to assess the underlying legal entity with which a contractual agreement is undertaken. Derivatives trading activities, for example, may be conducted through subsidiaries rather than the parent company.

Legal risk is more complex when it involves international financial operations, since foreign laws apply to many aspects of an organization's transactions. In international financial management, legal risk is closely related to sovereign risk, since the activities of the sovereign government may alter the legal rules under which transactions are undertaken. It is critical to obtain the advice of professionals in this area.

Sovereign or Country Risk

Sovereign or country risk arises from legal, regulatory, and political exposures in international transactions. Every nondomestic credit exposure consists of exposure to the credit quality of the entity or issuer and exposure to the credit quality and integrity of the sovereign nation where the issuer is domiciled.

Sovereign risk arises when transactions in other countries expose an organization to the restrictions and regulations of foreign governments. Even a counterparty or debt issuer with a high-quality credit rating can become problematic if the sovereign government makes it difficult to do business. Problems can arise with the issuer's ability to fulfill its own obligations in an environment that becomes financially or politically hostile.

From time to time, countries and governments have temporarily or permanently imposed controls on capital, prevented cross-border payments, suspended debt repayments, suspended convertibility of the currency, changed laws, and seized assets. Financial crises can sometimes precipitate, or be precipitated by, political turmoil, resulting in additional problems.

An organization with activities outside its borders should analyze sovereign risk and its exposure in those countries where it conducts business or maintains investments. Market intelligence about potential problems that is reasonably reliable from operations or contacts in other parts of the world should be monitored. Political and financial events can unfold quickly, and markets can move much more than would otherwise be expected.

Concentration Risk

Concentration risk affects organizations with exposure that is poorly diversified by region or sector, for example. Events or market changes may adversely affect all in an industry or sector. An organization that is diversified within a sector may still have poor diversification between sectors. As a result, the organization may suffer adversely if conditions worsen for those sectors.

A bank with a large number of borrowers in a particular industry sector is vulnerable to industry concentration risk. Similarly, an investment portfolio may be subject to concentration risk if it specializes in a particular industry or sector. Corporations affected by concentration risk include those with a customer base concentrated in a particular region, companies with one or two major customers, or significant real estate holdings with a single tenant.

Although counterparty and settlement risk are associated with transactions, concentration risk is associated with lack of diversification in exposure to countries, regions, or industries. Concentration risk, and therefore credit risk, is reduced through diversification of exposure.

Credit Exposure Management

A key credit risk management technique is the reduction of credit exposure. The techniques used depend to a certain degree on the type of organization. In general, there is more emphasis on active credit exposure management within financial institutions. This is not surprising given the importance of credit in the business of financial institutions as

IN THE REAL WORLD

Notable Quote

"Banking supervision, like counterintelligence, is hard to judge from the outside, because the success stories don't get told and the failures are on the front pages."

Source: Martin Mayer, *The Fed* (New York: The Free Press, Simon & Schuster, 2001), p. 237.

a result of lending, trading, and asset management activities. However, these are techniques that can be used by any organization.

Some techniques that are useful for managing credit exposure follow:

- Formalize the credit risk function.

- Consider opportunities for credit exposure diversification.

- Require settlement and payment techniques that provide certainty.

- Deal with high-quality counterparties.

- Use collateral where appropriate.

- Use netting agreements where possible.

- Monitor and limit market value of outstanding contracts.

Credit Risk Function

An independent risk management function, as discussed in Chapter 8, provides important strategic and tactical support to management and the board of directors. Credit risk management and policy development may be included in the risk oversight function or, in larger organizations, as a separate function.

The management of credit exposure should include setting appropriate credit exposure limits and monitoring and reporting exposures against limits on an aggregate, legally enforceable basis. Collateral and other credit enhancement techniques also belong within the risk management function, along with determining the method and frequency for reviewing credit policies.

Consistent with principles of portfolio management, both the credit risk of individual transactions and the credit risk of a portfolio of exposures should be considered.

Diversification

The concept of diversification can be illustrated with a traditional financial institution. Financial institutions were conventionally most affected by credit risk through their lending operations. The traditional relationship between a financial institution and a customer was nurtured by a relationship manager or account officer, with lending taking a central role.

Historically, financial institutions were often regional in nature and grew up near their customer base. The fortunes of both the customers and the regional financial institution, therefore, hinged on regional prosperity.

Lending was usually based on real assets such as equipment or, alternatively, real estate. In the event of a customer default on a loan, the financial institution could seize the pledged assets and obtain at least a partial recovery. The maximum credit exposure was the loan amount, and the risk depended on the borrower's likelihood of repayment.

In the traditional financial institution's lending model, credit committees ensured that credit risk resulting from banking activities such as lending was not excessive. Among other things, the customer's relationship with a financial institution and the community was often a key consideration in determining its likelihood to obtain credit. Financial institutions diversified to the extent possible, within the confines of their regional businesses and the regulatory environment.

Today many organizations face concentrated credit exposure. It may be difficult for organizations to diversify business activities adequately to reduce exposure. For example, a manufacturer may have many customers in the same industry. It may undesirable from a business perspective to diversify in an attempt to reduce this exposure to the industry, since these customers keep the manufacturer in business. However, management can recognize the concentration, seek ways to manage the exposure, and diversify as opportunities arise.

Credit Rationing

The business of credit rationing is as old as the banking business, but it is not exclusive to banking. The key tenet of credit rationing is that credit is granted where the most attractive risk-to-return tradeoff is available. This involves assigning higher interest rates to higher risk transactions to compensate for the additional risk. It also involves rationing the finite quantity of credit granted between borrowers with varying credit risk.

Financial institutions use credit committees to diversify credit-granting decisions and formalize the process. Credit scoring models are used by lenders to improve the ability to forecast default. Economic analysis and forecasting helps to predict economic conditions that might hinder expansion or increase default rates.

The tradeoff between risk and return is the basic premise for risk-adjusted return on capital (RAROC) models that are widely used. These models and derivatives of them are also used in budgeting and management decisions to assist in developing a portfolio that represents the best expected risk-adjusted return.

Collateral

Collateral has long been used to support various lending agreements. Derivatives exchanges, for example, have used collateral in the form of margin for decades. Exchanges require margin to initiate a derivatives transaction. In the event of a subsequent decline in value, additional margin may be required.

Collateral is being used with renewed interest in financial markets due to its risk-reduction potential. In the wholesale financial markets, the increased use of repurchase transactions (repos) illustrates the usefulness of collateralization as a risk reduction technique. Repos function as an alternative to noncollateralized lending or borrowing.

IN THE REAL WORLD

Collateral Use

Among derivatives dealers, there is an increased use of collateral. A 2004 International Swaps and Derivatives Association (ISDA) survey of collateral use in privately negotiated derivatives transactions and related margined activities found an increase in the volume of collateral of 41 percent over the previous year. The majority of the organizations using collateral are banks, and reduction of credit risk is a principal reason for its use.

A repo transaction consists of a sale transaction and a subsequent repurchase (sale-and-repurchase) or purchase-and-resale of securities, depending on the participant's perspective. Because title to the securities changes hands, the lender is effectively granted collateral over the term of the transaction, which may be as short as one day. Both the U.S. Federal Reserve and the Bank of Canada use repo transactions in their open market operations.

The requirement for collateral in a transaction can be dictated by a credit enhancement clause. The addition of such a clause in derivatives or lending transactions should be approached with caution, as the clause may apply to both counterparties. In the event of a credit worsening or significantly negative marked-to-market value in an outstanding position, an organization would be required to post additional collateral.

Netting Agreements

When a netting agreement is used, amounts to be exchanged between counterparties are netted, greatly reducing the counterparties' exposure to one another. Correctly undertaken, netting is one of the most important tools for managing credit exposure.

The development of netting agreements between counterparties has been instrumental in minimizing settlement risk, particularly in derivative transactions. The use of master agreements to cover most or all transactions between counterparties, such as an ISDA agreement, helps to set out the requirements for credit risk reduction. These agreements should apply to payments between counterparties and to close-out netting, which is used to close out a contract if a counterparty becomes bankrupt, for example.

Bilateral netting agreements, typically between two financial institutions, are used by many participants in the foreign exchange markets. Rather than make individual settlements between the counterparties, all payments for a given day and a currency pair are totaled and only the net payments are made.

Individual netting agreements may not entirely protect market participants if payments are still required to occur in different currencies, since payments may be made by both counterparties. However, the resulting payments will be smaller than they would otherwise be without netting, thus reducing exposure significantly.

Multilateral netting arrangements typically involve a group of organizations such as the participating financial institutions in CLS, discussed in more detail in Chapter 10. Many netting arrangements are supported by ISDA agreements for trading in swaps and other derivatives. Netting is also used among multinational corporations where multiple payments between the associated companies would otherwise take place.

Marking-to-Market

Marking-to-market is not a credit exposure management technique by itself but a tool used in conjunction with limits for reducing potential loss. Outstanding contracts that have large unrealized gains (unrealized losses for the counterparties) are monitored closely by periodic marking to market. The intent is to manage the potential for loss in the event of the failure or unwillingness of the counterparty to realize its losses. Gains and losses are compared to limits, and steps can subsequently be taken to protect the gains.

Marking-to-market may be combined with a pricing reset if the value of a contract goes beyond a predetermined limit. Alternatively, periodically renegotiating the contract at market value on a regular, prescheduled basis is another way to manage the risk of counterparty's default.

In the event that a counterparty's unrealized losses exceed a predetermined limit, a risk-mitigating action can be taken. This action may be a payment from the counterparty with losses to the counterparty with gains to "reset" the rate on the outstanding contract, creating a new marked-to-market value of zero in the example of an interest rate swap. Gains and losses are paid out and permitted to accrue for only a short period.

Alternatively, the counterparties may decide to close out the existing contracts at current market prices, settling as necessary, and re-enter similar contracts to replace them. There may be tax or legal ramifications of such transactions, however, and these should be understood.

Credit Limits

Traditional credit risk management techniques involve careful counterparty selection. Diversification of borrowers and counterparties includes selecting counterparties with a minimum acceptable credit quality and diversifying to avoid excessive exposure to any particular region, country, or industry. Limits assist in aggregate counterparty exposure management arising from both financial and business activity.

The use of limits supports and formalizes the principles of diversification. Limits are used in credit risk management as they are in asset management. A portfolio of weakly or negatively correlated exposures is expected to be less risky than a few highly correlated ones.

Financial institutions involved in trading actively use position limits to restrict the size of a trading position and the loss potential. Limits for individual traders and trading desks are set based on experience, performance, risk measurement and modeling, and the institution's risk tolerance, among other things. Both daylight limits (during the trading day) and overnight limits (for open positions and trading in foreign markets) are used. Many organizations and most banks also aggressively monitor counterparty limits on a worldwide, real-time, aggregate basis.

Contingent Actions

Contingent actions involve changes to an outstanding contract or agreement based on the occurrence of certain key events. Typically, these events are specified in a clause to a contractual agreement and might include the deterioration of a counterparty's credit quality, the

 TIPS & TECHNIQUES

Credit Limits

Organizations using derivatives or acting as industry creditors should consider counterparty or creditor, maximum contract size, or maximum term limits. Limits can be used to reduce exposure to sectors, regions, or sovereign governments. They may be included in investment policy statements, with acceptable issuer limits based on the ratings of major rating agencies. Country or sector limits may be used to minimize the exposure to a geographical region or industry.

marked-to-market value of an outstanding contract exceeding a predetermined amount, or both.

For example, if a counterparty's credit quality falls below a predetermined level, one or both parties may have the right to trigger a termination of the outstanding contract (sometimes known as a termination put), based on falling credit quality and significant changes in the value of the outstanding contract. Other credit enhancement clauses might specify the need for collateral to offset unrealized losses on an outstanding contract or for future contracts. Two-way payment provisions permit the parties to terminate the contract in the event of bankruptcy or similar.

Although a clause regarding a contingent action may give additional comfort in the event of a deterioration of credit quality, the end result of this action may be to worsen the credit impact for the counterparty. The result could lead to bankruptcy, adversely affecting all creditors. In addition, a clause added today may be used against an organization under circumstances that are not anticipated.

As a result, use of such clauses and follow-up action should be considered carefully, from a risk management standpoint and within permitted actions by local laws and regulations.

Other Credit Risk Management Techniques

Other credit exposure management techniques include secured lending transactions, where lending is secured with assets of value, and credit insurance, such as receivables insurance provided by a third party to protect against payment default.

Debt covenants are designed to protect creditors and require a borrower to maintain certain financial conditions. For example, a covenant may prohibit a borrower from paying dividends to common shareholders unless earnings are maintained above a predetermined level. Other covenants might limit debt to a specific percentage of capital.

Credit Derivatives

The emergence of credit derivatives offers a new mechanism for managing credit risk. Credit derivatives enable participants to offset risks that arise as a result of their core business or from an inability to diversify. Given the importance of credit risk, the market for credit derivatives is potentially larger than the market for other financial derivatives.

Participants in the global credit derivatives markets include financial institutions, governments, corporations, and fund managers. The largest participants in the credit derivatives markets are commercial and investment banks. A number of global financial institutions are active participants and make markets to others in various types of credit derivatives. Insurance and reinsurance companies and hedge funds are also participants in the credit derivatives market.

Credit derivatives are contractual agreements based on credit performance—typically swaps or options. Credit performance may be based on events such as default, insolvency or bankruptcy, nonpayment of loan obligations, or downgrading by a rating agency, for example. To be part of a contractual agreement, the event must be predetermined and readily identifiable when it occurs.

Credit derivatives can be classified according to the type of underlying credit that they are designed to hedge. The major credit categories are sovereign or country risk, financial institution risk, and corporate risk. A contract's underlying interest may be a particular credit name or a basket or portfolio of credit names. The terms *protection seller* and *protection buyer* are used commonly to differentiate the perspective of parties to a credit derivatives transaction.

Advantages of Credit Derivatives

Like other derivatives, credit derivatives provide a mechanism permitting the transfer of unwanted risk between willing counterparties, from organizations with too much credit risk, or the wrong type of credit risk, to organizations willing to assume it.

The credit derivatives business has similarities with the insurance underwriting business. In the credit derivatives business, the protection buyer seeks credit protection from the protection seller. There may be an outright exchange of risks, or one party may pay for risk reduction. Like the insurance business, changes to factors beyond management's control, such as weather or the economy, can result in increased or decreased claims and a resultant profit or loss.

Credit derivatives facilitate a portfolio approach to credit risk management and diversification. Changes to a credit portfolio can take time. A financial institution that perceives its credit portfolio to be too risky can enter into a contract to transfer some of its credit risk to another organization while it focuses on ways to refine the underlying portfolio.

Credit derivatives also allow market participants, especially financial institutions, to separate credit risk from market risk. There is an important distinction between credit risk and market risk. As a result, credit derivatives are useful in situations where credit risk needs to be mitigated without altering the underlying portfolio of transactions that initially created the risk.

The existence of credit derivatives provides some additional price transparency to the business of credit. Financial market participants may benefit from a better understanding of the value of credit even if they are not participants in the credit derivatives business.

Credit Default Swaps

The most common credit derivatives are credit default swaps, which have had significant increases in trading volumes and participants.

In a credit default swap, the protection seller makes a contingent payment to the protection buyer if a predetermined credit event occurs.

In exchange for assuming the credit exposure, the protection seller receives a premium that may be paid upfront or periodically (e.g., annually).

Credit default swaps specify the contingent credit event that must occur for compensation to be made, and therefore, it must be specifically and unambiguously outlined in the swap agreement. Although expressed with more clarity, the general nature of the credit event might be one of the following:

- Bankruptcy of the reference entity

- Restructuring of the reference entity

- Failure to pay by the reference entity

The underlying reference asset, such as a particular bond, is referenced in the contract and may be settled in cash or with delivery of the underlying reference asset. Depending on the agreement, the compensating payment from the protection seller to the protection buyer might be a fixed payment, a payment compensating for a partial recovery based on the contract's strike price, the underlying asset's par value, or an agreed-upon amount based on recovery, for example.

Other credit swaps designed to hedge a credit portfolio permit the protection buyer to receive compensation based on the first default that occurs in the underlying portfolio. This is known as a *first-to-default* basis.

Credit Spread Derivatives

Other credit derivatives are based on the interest rate differential between the debt of different types of issuers. A realized or expected rating change of an issuer will impact its cost of borrowing compared with a benchmark rate. All else being equal, a credit upgrade or improvement, particularly by one of the major rating agencies, will result in the ability to borrow at lower interest rates. Conversely, a credit downgrade will result in an increase in the cost of borrowing.

Credit spread derivatives may be structured as options or similar to forwards. A credit spread option requires upfront premium in exchange for protection against (typically) a widening credit spread between the underlying credit and a benchmark government yield, for example. The protection (put) buyer pays premium to the seller and in return receives a contingent payment if the spread widens past a predetermined level. With a credit spread forward, payment depends on whether the spread is above or below the contracted credit spread.

Since changes in the level of market interest rates should affect both the issuer and benchmark yields similarly, they should not affect credit swap payments unless there is also a change in relative credit spreads. A change in credit spreads will affect the value of the contract and therefore the obligations of counterparties to the contract.

Other Credit Derivatives

Other credit derivatives include total return swaps and credit-linked notes. Total return swaps involve an exchange of the total return from an underlying reference asset, such as a bond, against a predetermined fixed or variable reference rate. The total return from the asset includes

TIPS & TECHNIQUES

Spreadlocks

Spreadlocks are contractual agreements that protect an organization's ability to enter into an interest rate swap at a predetermined spread over government yields. In the event that the organization's credit quality declines, the spreadlock provides protection. Spreadlocks may be structured as forwards or options.

changes in value arising from market interest rates, changes to the issuer's credit rating, and the potential for default. One party receives the total return (comprising both market and credit gains or losses) and in exchange pays a predetermined return to the other.

Credit-linked notes are debt instruments with an embedded credit derivative. The investor receives par at maturity unless a predetermined credit event occurs (e.g., the reference credit defaults), in which case the investor receives less than par value (the recovery amount).

Credit Derivatives Challenges

Trading in credit derivatives has increased dramatically and has the potential to represent a significant proportion of all derivatives activity. Credit derivatives provide certain advantages to market participants that otherwise are difficult to obtain, including better transparency in the pricing of credit risk and the ability to diversify credit exposures.

Some critics charge, however, that rapid growth in credit derivatives presents particular risks. One concern is that market participants may become more aggressive in credit and counterparty transactions if they can transfer credit risks to someone else. Other criticisms include lack of transparency, potential pricing issues, and legal issues, particularly with cross-border transactions or reference credits. It has also been argued that, like other derivatives, credit derivatives spread risk around but don't actually reduce it, thus increasing systemic risk.

Modeling the probability of borrower default, and the potential for default correlations, like modeling the probability of market movements, is a science that is still being refined. It is critical to ensure that credit derivatives are priced accurately to reflect the underlying risk.

Liquidity remains another challenge. Although the number of dealers and trading volumes are growing, they are still relatively small. As a result, it may be difficult to find an appropriate counterparty to close out or offset an existing transaction, particularly in times of market stress or if the contract contains unusual terms.

The development of derivatives markets often precedes the legal and tax infrastructure to support them, and credit derivatives are no exception. Legal systems vary from country to country, and what constitutes law or legal precedence in one country may not be valid elsewhere. Credit derivatives may not have been subject to legal testing in all jurisdictions, and their potential overlap with insurance may also complicate matters in some legal systems.

Within an individual contract, clarity is very important. The definition of a credit event is critical in credit derivatives contracts. There may be complexities in deciding whether or not a contractual condition has been met, particularly if the underlying credit has operations in a number of legal jurisdictions or is rated by several rating agencies.

Although credit derivatives are specialized transactions, there is a need for standardization and documentation, which has been an important focus of ISDA.

TIPS & TECHNIQUES

ISDA Documentation

Credit derivatives have been an important focus of ISDA, an industry association made up of around 600 of the world's leading financial institutions. Among other risk management initiatives, ISDA provides standardized documentation that is used in a wide variety of derivatives transactions, including credit derivatives. These documents can be obtained directly from ISDA. Future efforts at standardization will further streamline trading and settlements for hedgers and traders.

Summary

- The credit risk component of financial risk management is significant due to interrelationships between global issuers, markets, and regions.

- Methods to reduce credit exposure include netting arrangements, marking to market, use of limits, and actions contingent on credit quality.

- Credit derivatives permit market participants to offset risks that arise as a result of their core business or as a result of difficulty in diversification.

CHAPTER 6

Commodity Risk

After reading this chapter you will be able to

- Describe the unique aspects of commodity-related risks
- Evaluate basic forward and futures strategies for managing commodity risk
- Identify additional strategies for managing commodity price risk

Not all financial risk arises directly from financial securities prices and rates. Commodity prices are a source of market risk and an important consideration for many organizations. Commodity price risk management is enhanced considerably by a variety of hedging products, while new frontiers in related risk management products include weather risk contracts, environmental credits, and derivatives on economic indicators.

Commodities are somewhat unusual in the risk management world. Unlike financial securities, commodities are physical assets with unique attributes. Commodities must be stored, and in many cases spoilage or deterioration is a concern. As a result, there are risk management considerations that do not apply to purely financial securities.

In some cases, commodity exposures are difficult to hedge effectively. There are several reasons why this might occur. There may be weak correlation between the exposure and the available hedge. Alternatively, the market for a particular commodity may not be large or liquid enough to warrant actively traded derivatives, and therefore underlying exposure may be difficult to hedge given the hedging products available. In certain markets, it may be difficult to sell commodities short, since short selling requires the ability to borrow the product.

In some markets, major participants may offer fixed prices to their customers that are similar to forward contracts. Other alternative risk management mechanisms exist, such as crop insurance for agricultural products that may provide a recovery of 25 to 50 percent of losses.

Commodity risk management permits producers to hedge against declining prices. Similarly, manufacturers and other users reduce the risk of rising prices by hedging. The final consumer benefits from price stability as a result of the ability to hedge price risk.

Managing commodity price risk requires an understanding of the nature of the commodity risk to which an organization is exposed and the products available to assist in developing a risk management strategy. A strategy can then be considered in light of the organization's priorities and risk tolerance.

Historical References

The Dojima rice market in Japan began trading in the early 1700s. Dojima traded rice futures contracts in 1730, predating North American exchanges by a century. Rice was a primary commodity in Japan at that time, and therefore its price was an important economic barometer.

In the mid–1800s, grain forward contracts were recorded in Chicago, and in 1848 the Chicago Board of Trade (CBOT) was established. Commodities markets grew as innovations such as margin and standardized contracts were instituted.

Fixed-Rate Contracts

The forerunners to traded derivatives contracts were fixed-rate contracts, which have been used by producers and merchants in one form or another for centuries. Today, some large commodities participants offer fixed-rate contracts to clients for hedging purposes. These private arrangements are alternatives to forward contracts, offering convenience and enabling smaller organizations or those in illiquid markets to obtain price protection.

The major advantage of a fixed-rate arrangement is the ease with which price protection is obtained. Contracts may be customized to permit the hedger to retain rights, such as the right to sell at current market prices if it is favorable to do so. Potential disadvantages of fixed-rate contracts include their lack of liquidity and any potential contractual limitations, such as the requirement to use the existing agreement for new purchases to maintain the relationship. In many markets, buyers have the power to set favorable contractual terms, while in other markets sellers command favorable terms.

Types of Participants

Participants in the commodities markets generally fall into one of two broad classifications. Dealers make prices to others and often trade speculatively. End users and suppliers are in the commodity business, directly or indirectly, and usually hedge to protect against price and supply fluctuations. These main market participants are:

- *Commodity dealers that are active market participants on behalf of their own organizations or clients.* Dealers include financial institutions, major commodity producers, commodity trading houses, and commodity trading advisors (CTAs). Speculators exploit arbitrage opportunities or inefficiencies and in doing so provide additional liquidity.

- *Consumers of commodities, including manufacturers, refineries, and wholesalers.* Commodity consumers are exposed to rising commodities prices that increase costs of manufacture or production and reduce profit.

- *Suppliers of commodities, including farmers and growers, and mining and exploration companies.* Suppliers typically require protection against decreases in the market price of a commodity that reduce revenues. Commodity producers often cite commodity price risk as the most critical factor to their economic survival.

Since commodity prices influence production revenues, they also influence decisions about production. Below a threshold commodity price level, producers may reduce existing production or curtail new production. When commodity prices rise, production that was previously only marginally profitable may become attractive, resulting in increased production levels. As a result of the production decision, both demand and supply are affected by significant price changes. The value of inventory is also a consideration.

IN THE REAL WORLD

Commodity Exposures

Energy prices are a key exposure for many companies. A survey of members of the Association of Corporate Treasurers published in 2003 by Ernst & Young[a] found that exposure to oil and gas was the most common commodity exposure, followed by electricity prices and base metals prices.

[a] "Which Path Are You On?" Treasury Operations Survey, Ernst & Young, 2003.

Commodities Markets

In addition to over-the-counter commodity derivatives markets, a number of major commodities exchanges offer futures and option products. The market continues to grow with new products such as economic statistic and weather derivatives gaining acceptance among hedgers and speculators.

Metals

The precious metals are gold, silver, platinum, and palladium. In terms of volume traded, the largest exchange for precious metals futures contracts is the COMEX division of the New York Mercantile Exchange (NYMEX).

In addition to their use in industry, precious metals—and gold in particular—are deemed to be a store of wealth and an inflation hedge. Market participants buy precious metals in anticipation of rising inflation, pushing up prices. Precious metals also have a high emotional impact since they have often been a safe-haven asset in times of financial or political upheaval. In addition, prices are subject to market influences such as interest rates and inflation.

Industrial metals include copper, tin, aluminum, nickel, zinc, and lead. Although silver is sometimes included as an industrial metal, it is usually considered to be a precious metal.

Agricultural Commodities

Agricultural commodities can be divided into several categories, including soft commodities, grains, livestock, and oilseeds. The major agricultural products, as measured by U.S. exchange trading volumes, are corn, soybeans, sugar, and soybean oil.

IN THE REAL WORLD

Breakfast in New York

In addition to cotton, breakfast staples such as coffee, sugar, cocoa, and frozen concentrated orange juice trade at the New York Board of Trade (NYBOT), which comprises three historic exchanges:

- Coffee, Sugar, and Cocoa Exchange

- New York Cotton Exchange

- New York Futures Exchange

Grains

Grains are a key commodity group due to their ability to feed humans and livestock. Important grains include rice, wheat, canola, oats, and corn, as well as rye and barley.

There are two major categories of grains based on their use:

- Feed grains are used for feeding livestock.

- Food grains are used for human consumption. Corn is unique in that it is used both as a feed grain and a food grain.

The demand for food grain is influenced greatly by requirements for food manufacture and from other nations that require more than they produce domestically. Drought or crop failure can reduce supplies in other countries, causing higher than normal demand as grain is purchased by those needing to make up their own shortfall. The supply of food grain is affected by weather and natural disaster, as well as advances in crop yields and genetic engineering.

Wheat has the largest volume production of the food grains. Major wheat producers include Eastern Europe, the European Union, China, India, United States, Canada, Australia, and Argentina, although it is grown in almost every region of the world. One of wheat's most important uses is in the production of flour.

Livestock

The Chicago Mercantile Exchange (CME) offers trading in live animals and related animal product. The CME introduced the first futures contract on live cattle in 1964. Currently, it lists futures and options on futures on feeder cattle, live cattle, and lean hogs.

Oilseeds

Soybeans are the most actively traded oilseed commodity in terms of trading activity and volume. In addition to trading soybean contracts, market participants also trade the crush spread to lock in the processing spread, since soybeans are crushed or processed to produce soybean oil

IN THE REAL WORLD

Trading the Weather

Weather derivatives enable organizations to hedge against adverse weather conditions that affect business and profitability. Users include utilities, insurance companies, and governments such as municipalities. The most common temperature-based weather derivatives use heating degree days (HDD) and cooling degree days (CDD), both of which measure average daily temperature against a benchmark of 65 degrees Fahrenheit.

and soybean meal. This is done by simultaneously buying soybean contracts and selling oil and meal contracts on a predetermined ratio basis.

Canola and flaxseed are also considered oilseeds. Although the price spread between the two varies considerably, there is a fundamental price relationship based on the price for the protein meal and the derivative oil, and hedgers also pay close attention to this relationship as well as to market prices.

Energy

The energy market is one of the most sophisticated commodities markets. As a result of energy price volatility, new products have continually evolved. Products trade in both the exchange-traded market and the over-the-counter market. Energy swaps, options, futures, forwards, and more complex derivatives are used by participants with increasing volumes. Price and supply are very important, and energy prices impact many other markets. Petroleum products, for example, affect the manufacturing cost of various products such as plastics and resins.

NYMEX offers contracts in a number of energy products, including the following:

- Heating oil

- Light sweet crude oil

- Brent crude oil

- Unleaded gasoline

- Natural gas

- Electricity

- Propane

- Coal

IN THE REAL WORLD

Electricity Trading

Electricity differs from other commodities in that it cannot be readily stored. An actively traded market, electricity can exhibit significant price volatility, in particular since electricity is essential to power the technology of modern civilization. In some regions, the adjustments related to deregulation have contributed to price volatility. Electricity contracts trade in the over-the-counter market and on NYMEX, where they are cash settled.

The control of energy such as petroleum brings political and economic power, and as a result, it is subject to political maneuvers that affect prices. The early development of energy hedging products was influenced significantly by volatility arising out of turmoil in the Middle East, as greater price volatility increased demand for protection.

Other Commodities

Other commodities contracts trade both on and off exchanges. Contracts for random-length lumber and fertilizer are listed on the CME. Peanuts trade on the Beijing Commodity Exchange in China, raw silk on the Kobe Raw Silk Exchange in Japan, and rubber on the Singapore Commodity Exchange.

Commodity Forwards and Futures

A forward contract is an agreement between a buyer and a seller to exchange a commodity at a predetermined price on a future delivery date. Both the buyer and seller are obligated by the forward once it has been transacted.

A futures contract is a standardized forward contract that trades on an exchange. Performance by counterparties to a futures contract is guaranteed by a clearing corporation, while a forward contract is not.

Commodity forward and futures contracts provide similar protection from commodity price fluctuations. Forwards trade in the over-the-counter market with delivery dates and amounts customized. Related products include contracts for difference.

In the United States, the Commodity Futures Trading Commission (CFTC) is the federal agency that regulates commodity futures and options markets.

Forward Pricing

The price of a commodity for future delivery differs from the cash price by an amount known as the basis. The basis consists of carrying charges associated with owning the commodity, such as storage, interest charges on money borrowed to buy the commodity, and insurance. The basis may be positive or negative.

In a normal or contango market, the forward or futures price is higher than the cash price to accommodate the cost of carrying (owning) the commodity from the trade date to delivery. Included in this cost are financing costs, insurance, and storage costs. When demand for the commodity for immediate delivery is high, market participants push up prices for near-term delivery. A backwardation or inverted market is one that exhibits higher prices for near-term delivery than for longer-term delivery.

If the basis is not reflective of carrying charge factors, speculators could buy the cash commodity and hold it, selling an offsetting futures contract and eventually delivering against it to earn arbitrage profits. Delivery is the link between forward or futures prices and cash prices, and presuming the same delivery location and underlying product, these prices converge as contract expiry approaches, eliminating the basis entirely by delivery.

Forward Prices

The following prices for gold futures contracts illustrate a normal market, where the farthest delivery prices are higher than near-term delivery prices:

December	$430.80
February	$432.60
April	$434.40
June	$436.30

Commodities prices, and forward and futures prices on commodities, are also affected by weather, political stability, perception of shortages, the availability of substitutes, and shifting consumer tastes.

Using Commodity Futures Contracts

An organization with exposure to commodity prices can use futures or forward contracts to manage its exposure. Exchange-traded transactions are conducted through a broker that acts as an intermediary between buyer and seller, while transactions are conducted directly between counterparties or through an inter-dealer broker in the over-the-counter market.

The purchase of a futures or forward contract protects against rising prices of the underlying commodity. The contract may be used for delivery or closed out and delivery taken through normal channels. When the commodity price rises, gains in the value of the futures contract should offset the higher commodity cash purchase price. If the commodity price declines, the futures contract will incur losses that should offset the lower commodity cash purchase price.

The contract reduces the risk of adverse price movements to both buyer and seller for future delivery but does not address basis risk. The basis is the difference between the cash price and the forward price and may result from differences in delivery date, location, or other factors. A shift in the basis, where the pricing relationship has changed, can adversely or favorably impact the performance of a hedge. As a result, the hedge may be imperfect, with resultant residual risk. The basis should be taken into account in assessing the likely effectiveness of a hedge before it is undertaken. In some cases, the hedge may not be effective enough to undertake.

Futures contracts trade with standardized delivery dates and specifications, the deliverable quality or grade of commodity, and contract sizes. If an outstanding contract is not offset with another prior to expiry, the seller may deliver the commodity during the allowable delivery period, as permitted by the exchange. Contracts may be based on the physical commodity or on a commodity basket or index.

Delivery

A small percentage of futures contracts involve delivery. Most futures contracts are offset prior to expiry. Many hedgers find the futures contract works adequately as a hedge, and at expiry the futures contract is offset with another (i.e., closed out or rolled forward). The sale or purchase of commodity is then transacted through normal, often local, channels.

For exchange-traded contracts, the exchange determines commodity or quality deliverable against the contract. The seller of the futures contract determines the delivery from the allowable attributes stipulated by the exchange. Exchange against physical may be possible.

Some contracts, such as NYMEX electricity and most index contracts, are cash-settled. At the contract's expiry date, the buyer and the

IN THE REAL WORLD

Deliverable Grades

The following are deliverable grades of corn and price adjustments as stipulated by the CBOT, for the 5,000-bushel corn futures contract:

- No. 2 yellow at par

- No. 1 yellow at 1 $\frac{1}{2}$ cents per bushel over contract price

- No. 3 yellow at 1 $\frac{1}{2}$ cents per bushel under contract price

seller exchange cash based on the value of their net positions. The result is that the contract holder with a profit is compensated by the contract holder with a loss.

Mark-to-Market and Margin

The purchase or sale of a futures contract requires margin to be posted. Margin is a performance bond consisting of cash deposited with the futures broker. Minimum initial and maintenance margin requirements are set by the exchange and depend on the contract and the type of trade. Brokers may require additional margin from their customers for futures trades. The margin account is adjusted daily as contracts are marked to market to reflect changes in the value of the futures position.

Calculating a Local Basis

The difference between a local cash market price for a commodity and the current or near futures contract price is known as a local basis. This basis may be negative or positive. Hedging a physical commodity with a standardized futures contract may lead to an imperfect hedge if local

TIPS & TECHNIQUES

Price Limits

Trading in futures contracts is governed by exchange regulations. Where they exist, daily price limits permit a maximum price fluctuation during a trading session. Limits may be waived during the month of delivery, since the activity of this near-date contract is likely to closely mimic the cash market. A contract is said to be limit up or limit down if it has reached its upper price limit or lower price limit, respectively.

Price limits temporarily insulate the market from panic related to major news, giving market participants time to assess new information. In addition, they help exchanges determine margin requirements, since a one-day maximum loss on open positions can be calculated. If futures contracts are being used for hedging, during times of significant price moves it is possible that prices might not completely reflect the cash or forward market due to these limits.

The following daily price limits, above or below the previous settlement, apply to agricultural products traded on the Winnipeg Commodity Exchange:

Canola	$30.00 per metric tonne
Flaxseed	$20.00 per metric tonne
Western barley	$7.50 per metric tonne
Domestic feed wheat	$7.50 per metric tonne

commodity prices do not move exactly with the futures prices. There may be a local basis to prices due to seasonal or quality variations or different delivery points.

Compilation of a historical average basis by tracking the difference between local cash prices and the nearby (current) futures price may be useful in determining the effectiveness of the hedge. This tracking can be done by observation or data collection over several months or years or, alternatively, by obtaining the information from external sources, if available. Local price basis data are calculated and published for some commodities and regions by news and information services.

Change in the Basis

A lumber producer wants to ensure a selling price for the delivery of its product in three months' time. With cash prices at $342 per thousand feet, and futures prices at $348 per thousand feet, the mill sells a lumber futures contract at $348 per thousand feet. The difference between cash and futures prices of $6 is the basis.

When the mill is ready to ship lumber, it buys back an offsetting futures contract, and delivers its lumber to its regular customers. However, cash prices have fallen to $332 per thousand feet, while the futures price is $339.

The fall in cash prices has caused a loss on the sale of the lumber of $10 per thousand feet. However, the futures contract has fallen only $9 per thousand feet of lumber. The basis has widened from $6 to $7 per thousand feet, which impacts the mill negatively. Although the hedge was mostly effective in protecting against falling, the change in the basis represents a difference of $1 per thousand feet.

The loss could have been a gain had the basis narrowed rather than widening, or it could have resulted in a larger loss. Although the basis shifted, the producer has benefited from protection at the futures price of $348.

Spreads

Spreads permit hedgers and speculators to trade the differences between contracts and are commonly used in the commodities markets. There are three basic types of spreads:

1. *Intra-market spreads,* which involve the purchase and sale of contracts for two different delivery dates

2. *Inter-market spreads,* which involve the purchase and sale of contracts on different exchanges with the same delivery dates

3. *Inter-commodity spreads,* which involve the purchase and sale of contracts for different commodities for the same delivery dates

Inter-commodity spreads can involve commodities and their derivative products. For example, the crack spread is a strategy that permits the difference between the price of crude oil and its refined products to be hedged, permitting hedgers to manage the refining spread.

Other inter-commodity spreads include:

- Frac spread, involving natural gas and propane

- Crush spread, involving soybeans and the derivative products soybean oil and soybean meal

- Spark spread, involving natural gas and electricity

Closing Out a Commodity Futures Contract

Most futures contracts are closed out prior to delivery, while many forward contracts are used for delivery. A futures or forward contract can be closed out in one of several ways:

- Take or make delivery per the terms of contract, or within exchange for physical provisions.

- Close out contract by buying/selling an offsetting contract at prevailing market rates.

- Extend or roll the contract to a future date.

A purchased contract can be offset with the sale of a contract with the same delivery and specifications as the original. Similarly, a sold contract would be offset with a purchased contract prior to expiry. A hedger may use a futures contract as price protection in a related product but have no interest in the commodity itself.

A hedger will earn a net gain or loss on the futures or forward contract, which should offset losses or gains on the actual commodity exposure. The effectiveness of the hedge depends on several factors, including the relationship between futures prices and the underlying exposure (the basis) and the number of contracts used to hedge (the hedge ratio). A significant difference between the exposure and the futures contract may result in being underhedged or overhedged.

TIPS & TECHNIQUES

Commodity Swaps

Commodity swaps enable hedgers to swap production or consumption prices against the return on an index or another market. They are popular over-the-counter products, with the largest volumes in energy and metals swaps. Market makers are typically commodity dealers and financial institutions.

A commodity swap may be relatively simple or complex. Virtually any type of swap can be modified as a commodity swap. For example, an oil producer can swap its oil production price for the return on another index, such as a fixed income yield.

The seller of a futures contract can also deliver the commodity against the contract. However, most contracts are closed out with offsetting contracts rather than physical delivery taken. Physical distances may make delivery impractical and costly. Exchange for physical provisions may permit buyers and sellers to negotiate price and delivery.

Commodity Options

A commodity option provides the option buyer with the right, but not the obligation, to buy or sell a specified (notional) amount of a commodity at the strike or exercise price. In exchange for this right, the option buyer pays option premium to the option seller. The writer (seller) of the option has the obligation to deliver, or accept delivery of, the underlying if the option buyer exercises it.

Commodity options trade between institutions in the over-the-counter market and in the exchange-traded market. Exchange-traded or listed options are transacted through a broker or futures commodity merchant and have standardized expiry dates, contract amounts, and strike prices.

Commodity options may have as their underlying either a physical commodity or a futures contract. The underlying futures contract may be based on a commodity index or the physical commodity. A commodity futures contract simplifies the delivery process as compared with physical delivery.

A put option gives the option buyer the right to sell the underlying commodity or futures contract at the strike price. Similarly, a call option gives the option buyer the right to buy the underlying commodity or futures contract at the strike price.

An American-style option is exercisable by the option holder any time until expiry. A European-style option is exercisable by the option holder on the expiry date, and therefore costs less than an American-

Options on
Futures Contracts

The following are sample call option prices for options on natural gas futures contracts as traded at the NYMEX. The underlying futures contract is 10,000 MMBtu (million British thermal units) for Louisiana (United States) delivery:

Strike Price	December	January	February
560.00	2.355	2.941	3.023
565.00	2.305	2.893	2.977
570.00	2.255	2.845	2.933
575.00	2.206	2.797	2.887

style option, all else being equal. From the option seller's standpoint, a European-style option involves less uncertainty than an American-style option, since the European-style cannot be exercised prior to expiry.

Over-the-counter options are traded by financial institutions, trading houses, and major commodity market participants, among others. These options are customized to the hedger's requirements with respect to expiry date, notional amount, underlying interest, and strike price.

Pricing Options

The relationship between an underlying commodity's market price and the option's strike price is a key determinant of the option's price. The favorable difference between the strike price and the market price, if any, is the option's intrinsic value. Intrinsic value is positive or zero.

A commodity option price is based on the following variables:

- Current commodity or underlying price

- Exercise privileges (e.g., American-style or European-style)

- Risk-free domestic interest rate

- Volatility of the price of the underlying commodity or futures contract

- Exercise or strike price

- Time until option expiration

An option that is at-the-money allows its holder to transact at current market (spot or forward) prices. An in-the-money option can be exercised by the option holder at better than current market prices. An out-of-the-money strike price is one that is less attractive than current market prices.

Relationship between Strike Price and Market Price	Call Option	Put Option
Strike price = Market price	At-the-money	At-the-money
Strike price less than market price	In-the-money	Out-of-the-money
Strike price greater than market price	Out-of-the-money	In-the-money

The relationship between the strike price and the market price is important because it is one determinant of an option's premium. This relationship also determines how the option's value is likely to change given a change in the underlying commodity price (the option's delta). The change in an option's value depends in part on the relationship of the strike price to market prices. The more that an option's strike price is out-of-the-money, the less likely it will be exercisable prior to expiry, and therefore the less its value will respond to changes in the price of the underlying.

When an option is purchased for hedging purposes, it is possible that the underlying commodity price will move adversely but not enough to make the option worthwhile exercising (i.e., the option remains out-of-the-money). In that case, the option will expire worthless, resulting in a loss from the underlying commodity price change and a loss on the option premium paid.

When an option is sold as an alternative to a hedge, the option premium received acts as a buffer against market movements. However, the sold option does nothing to protect the option seller from adverse market movements. Option sellers need to manage the risks associated with sold options actively.

Buying Options

An organization that has exposure to rising commodity prices can purchase a call option to provide it with protection above a predetermined strike price. For commodity producers or those with exposure to falling commodity price, the purchase of a put option provides protection below a predetermined strike price.

With the purchase of an option, the option buyer knows that the commodity price will not be worse than the option's strike price. The option premium paid is the price of the protection offered by the option.

Selling Options

The sale of options differs from the purchase of options. The seller receives option premium and accepts an obligation to buy or sell the commodity under the terms of the option, should the option be exercised. The decision to exercise the option is that of the option buyer.

Option premium provides a buffer against further adverse commodity price changes but does not hedge the commodity price risk. The premium received depends on the factors that affect an option's price, including volatility and time to expiry.

The option seller must actively manage the exposure and may have to take alternative measures if commodity prices move adversely. The

Selling Options

The decision to sell an option should not be based on whether levels of volatility and time value are attractive but on whether the risk-reward profiles of the strategy are reasonable and make sense. The option seller should monitor the position very closely, since a sold option alone does not constitute a hedge. A hedger that relies on a sold option to complete a hedge may find that the market moves adversely and the sold option is never exercised. The result is that no protection from adverse price movements is provided. Similarly, a speculative sold option may result in large or theoretically unlimited losses if not managed actively.

risks associated with selling an unhedged call option are theoretically unlimited. The risks associated with selling an unhedged put option are also high, although prices presumably can fall only to zero.

The sale of a commodity option involves a maximum gain of the premium received from the sale of the option. The option premium reduces the effective price for a commodity buyer and increases the effective price for a commodity seller. However, large or potentially unlimited losses can result, since the sale of an option alone does not provide protection against adverse price changes.

Commodity Collar

The purchase of options for hedging purposes is often costly. As a result, options are often packaged together as a collar to reduce hedging costs but still provide protection against an adverse price change. In exchange for protection against adverse prices, the hedger limits the potential for better prices using a collar.

Also known as a fence or range forward, the collar involves the purchase of an option and the sale of another option on the same underlying commodity and for the same contractual expiry date. The sold option generates option premium to pay for the purchased option, reducing or eliminating the option premium and the cost of the hedge.

An organization wanting to hedge against falling commodity prices can structure a collar by buying a put option and simultaneously selling a call option. If the commodity price falls, the hedger will exercise the put and sell the underlying commodity at the strike price, while the sold call will not be exercised. If the commodity price rises above the call strike price, the buyer of the call will exercise it and pay the hedger the call strike price for the commodity, while the put is unexercised. As a result, the hedger is protected against a worst-case price (the put strike price, in this example), and the cost of the hedge is funded by limiting the hedger's ability to take advantage of favorable prices above the call strike price.

Closing Out a Commodity Option

Whether to exercise an in-the-money option or close it out often depends on convenience and the reasons for buying the option in the first place. The holder of an option can exercise it (if it is in-the-money) or allow it to expire (if it is out-of-the-money). If an option has intrinsic or time value it can also be sold.

For sold options, the only way to close out the associated obligation is to buy back an offsetting option, which can be expensive if the market has moved against the option seller or if the option is in-the-money. If the sold option is not bought back, the obligation exists because the option holder may still exercise it any time according to the terms of the contract.

Alternatively, the seller of an option can deliver or accept delivery of the underlying commodity at the strike price, per the obligation imposed by the sale of the option, should the option be exercised by the option holder.

If the option is out-of-the-money, it is not likely to be exercised, and it is worthless at expiry. The option seller will keep the option premium, which reduces the effective cost of, or increases the effective selling price for, commodity transactions.

Summary

- Commodities are physical assets with unique attributes, unlike financial securities.

- A number of strategies exist for managing commodity price risk, including forwards and futures, swaps, and options.

- Commodity derivatives trade between institutions in the over-the-counter and the exchange-traded market.

- The basis represents a source of risk in commodity hedging. Some commodities exposures may be difficult to hedge without incurring significant basis risk.

CHAPTER 7

Operational Risk

After reading this chapter you will be able to

- Understand the prevalence of operational risk
- Identify situations in which operational risk is likely to be an issue
- Evaluate opportunities to reduce operational risk

O perational exposures arise from the possibility of fraud, error, or system or procedural problems. Methods to manage operational risk include clear financial risk management policy, documentation of policies and procedures, adequate risk oversight, and segregation of duties. Employee compensation, education and training, holidays, and job rotation policies are also important. These issues are discussed in the following pages.

Financial risk management primarily deals with the risks that arise directly or indirectly as a result of financial markets. Analysis of previous significant losses suggests that losses often occur as a result of one or more major problems:

- Speculative trading
- Unauthorized trading
- Not hedging
- Overhedging

- Poor processes

- Inadequate division of duties

- Lack of oversight

Other contributors to risk include:

- Merger situations—risks may be hard to manage during implementation phase

- Risk across an organization, particularly if there are separate suborganizations

How Operational Risk Arises

Operational risk arises from the activities of an organization in three key areas: people, processes, and technology. Many large derivatives losses have been exacerbated by, or resulted from, operational failings that permitted losses to accumulate.

IN THE REAL WORLD

Risk and Oversight

"The risk management mechanism at the Daiwa Bank was not effectively functioning, and directors failed to meet their oversight responsibility."

Conclusions of a Japanese court in the largest shareholder lawsuit ever filed against individuals in Japan ordered Daiwa executives to pay $775 million in damages for failure to oversee a New York–based trader who engaged in unauthorized bond trading and hiding of $1.1 billion in losses.

Operational risk has traditionally been loosely defined and quantified. The ability to manage operational risk requires knowledge of processes, systems, and personnel and the ability to ensure that duties and procedures have been clearly established, documented, and followed. Many risks that an organization faces cross risk boundaries—for example, combining credit risk and operational risk.

Although operational risk is usually associated with treasury or trading operations, these risks and exposures also exist in other types of organizations. Operational losses do not always occur in organizations with large volumes or complex operations. The complexities of financial products, volatility of financial markets, combined with the operational intricacies of an organization, can produce risks that need to be managed carefully in all organizations.

For corporations, the decline in market value of the company as a result of an operational failure, such as might occur as a result of

IN THE REAL WORLD

Controlling Operational Risk

Although the business of financial institutions and nonfinancial institutions differs significantly, many of the operational risks they face are similar. In past interviews by the Bank for International Settlements of about 30 major banks, internal controls and the internal audit process were seen by virtually all as the primary means to control operational risk.

Source: Risk Management Subgroup of the Basel Committee on Banking Supervision, "Operational Risk Management," September 1998.

declines in a publicly traded company's share price, may be greater than the actual operational losses. The perception of operational weaknesses is particularly negative.

In some cases, operational risk may be partially offset by insurance designed to meet the needs of specific operational failures or breakdowns. It is presumed that insurance is an important part of any risk management strategy, though its discussion is beyond our scope. However, the discussion will focus on conditions within an organization that may reduce the likelihood of an operational issue, where possible.

TIPS & TECHNIQUES

Operational Controls

Some suggestions for implementing operational controls are:

- Involve management with oversight and adequate information.

- Implement appropriate policies and procedures, including limits, controls, and reporting requirements. These should be documented.

- Set up an independent risk management function to ensure that policies and limits are not violated and to provide oversight to management.

- Use internal audits to ensure activities are consistent with policies.

- Include an administrative or support function that can independently price and report on transactions, if no risk oversight function exists.

152

Error and Fraud

People are critical to the functioning of an organization, and from a risk management perspective, they often represent one of its most significant risks.

Transactions involve employee decisions and relationships. As a result, potential for error and fraud must always be guarded against. Due to the size and volume of treasury and finance transactions, the potential damage of a large error or fraud is serious. In addition, personnel may be subject to pressure to outperform or earn profits, which exacerbates the risk of a problem. The risk of errors or fraud as a result of one or more individuals falls into this arena.

In addition to fraud perpetrated within an organization, there is also the risk of fraud by those external to the organization. Although it is beyond the scope of this discussion, scams have involved fraudulent financial securities, financial institutions, and contractual agreements, among others.

Processes and Procedures

Processes and procedures help to ensure that an organization's polices are followed. Documentation of policies and procedures may reduce administrative time and provide tactical support to employees.

Risk arising from processes and procedures includes the risk of adverse consequences as the result of missing or ineffective processes, procedures, controls, or checks and balances. Often, these processes are designed to catch error or fraud. Process and procedural risk affects hedging and trading decisions, the oversight and risk control functions, how transactions are processed, and adherence to policies.

Technology and Systems

Technology and systems risks are operational risks that arise from financial instrument pricing and trading systems, reliance on technology,

Unauthorized Trading

One potentially significant result of operational exposure is unauthorized or excessive trading, and the potential resultant losses.

One leading Lloyds of London syndicate developed an *unauthorized trading* insurance policy for large financial institutions. The policy was designed to provide coverage in the event of losses from unauthorized, concealed, or false trading in excess of a predetermined limit, trading in unauthorized instruments, or trading with unauthorized counterparties.

payments systems, protection of data and networks, and access to files or data that can be fraudulently altered.

The existence of technology has eased many of the mundane functions associated with treasury, cash management, and trading, but it introduces new challenges with respect to risk management. To a certain extent, the degree of operational risk arising from technology depends on the processes conducted inhouse. A financial institution may have a very different set of technology and processes to support it than a municipal government, for example. However, there are some common areas of exposure.

Systems and networks should be evaluated in light of their vulnerability to sabotage, fraud, or error. A complex system that is understood by only one employee is a temptation to problems. The subject of risk in technology and systems security is relatively technical, and many aspects are best suited for discussion with an industry professional.

An organization using financial products should have the technological ability to analyze the risks inherent in those products and the underlying exposure. If staff do not have access to appropriate technology, it will be difficult to manage the complexities of pricing and analysis of financial risk.

Operational Considerations

Operational risk encompasses people, processes, and technology, and its management requires consideration of operational issues. A few operational considerations may be useful:

- Maintain cash forecasts for various currencies and keep them current.

- Ensure employees have an opportunity for training and skills enhancement.

- Consider implementing job sharing or cross training to enhance team.

- Ensure adequate reporting to team, management, and board.

- Determine backups of both key data and employee roles.

- Maintain good relationships with financial institutions and other vendors.

- Ensure appropriate controls to guard against illegal activities, including money laundering.

Managing operational risk relies on the following tools:

- Contingent processing capability if the business relies on payment or other data processing

- Well-developed internal controls

- Use of internal audit

- Exception reporting for items that are missed, errors, or otherwise noteworthy

Different laws and regulations apply to different kinds of organizations around the world. Some of the following considerations may be addressed, or even restricted, by local laws and regulations, others not at all. This discussion is intentionally general in the sense that it presumes any operational issues will be undertaken within the more stringent laws and rules of either the local environment or the home country.

Internal Controls

Internal controls are perhaps the most important tools for managing operational risk. In fact, many large losses at banks can be attributed to internal control failures. The board of directors has final responsibility for ensuring that appropriate internal controls are implemented. Effectiveness of internal controls should periodically be tested and amended as necessary.

Appropriate division or segregation of duties among staff members is a key internal control. For example, confirmation should be separate from trading. Risk management reporting should be separate from trading. Separation may require an administrative or support function that can independently price and report on transactions when no formal risk oversight function exists. Other important control structures include approvals, reconciliations, and verifications.

One of an organization's greatest vulnerabilities comes from the potential for errors and fraud. If losses can be concealed, and an employee is tempted to do so because of pressure to generate profits or for other reasons, the organization is at tremendous risk, particularly since the largest losses are likely to be concealed with great effort.

The subject of internal control is complex and beyond the scope of this brief discussion. An adequate, effective audit program, monitoring, and a clear audit trail, in part derived from appropriate processes and reporting, is also critical. Liaison with professionals with audit, tax, and legal expertise is encouraged.

Compensation of Personnel

An organization that does not wish to speculate on financial market movements should not motivate its employees to speculate. However, even when employee compensation is based on something other than correct market forecasts, there may be subtle or implicit messages that accurate market forecasts are a definition of good performance. All managers should be able to identify opportunities to encourage the behavior that is warranted under the circumstances.

An appropriate compensation structure for finance personnel should suit the risk tolerance of the organization. Performance for bonuses should be considered carefully. Compensation is an important signal of performance expectations, particularly in the treasury department, where the process of mark-to-market is ongoing.

Finance personnel who are compensated with a profit-derived bonus are more likely to be motivated to take risks in pursuit of enhancement of the organization's (and their own) bottom line. Staff should know what is expected of them, and their compensation should reflect these expectations. An industrial company that does not wish to speculate in financial markets will want compensation based on something other than correct market bets.

Likelihood of fraud increases with employees in serious financial difficulty or with addictions such as gambling or drugs. Prospective employees should be screened carefully to the extent permissible by law to avoid potential problems.

Management Involvement

Management oversight and accountability is extremely important. Involvement of key management, as well as internal and external audit professionals, can also offer guidance in the area of controls. Management must have an appropriate level of knowledge about organizational risks to develop policies and acceptable strategies and monitor compliance.

In addition, deficiencies highlighted by audit or review should be corrected immediately, and feedback should ensure that problems have been corrected.

Conflicts of Interest

Management should be aware of the potential for conflicts of interest. If staff are influenced to transact business with certain institutions, these influences may have an impact on the independence of decisions made by staff. Although most finance professionals are familiar with issues of conflict, senior management should communicate exactly what is expected of treasury and finance personnel. This is especially true with respect to professional relationships with others in the business.

Both actual and perceived conflicts of interest should be considered. For example, employees have been encouraged to do business with a financial institution in exchange for preferential treatment for themselves or family members. This puts the organization's welfare in conflict with that of the employee and does not put the interests of stakeholders first. Some organizations prohibit personal transactions with dealers and financial institutions that do business with the organization to reduce potential for conflict.

Staff Training and Skills

Knowledgeable, well-rounded staff are an asset to any organization. Employees should be provided with opportunities for training and skills enhancement. This may require a dedicated training budget or allocation, as well as management support for training.

Employees should be encouraged to learn about other financial activities of the organization. Cross training is an opportunity to broaden employee skills and enhance a team, facilitate succession planning, avoid reliance on one or two key individuals, and ensure that other employees can step in quickly in the event of a sudden departure. Employee rotation may also make it harder for employees to cover up inappropriate actions, thus potentially reducing the likelihood of fraud, intentional misinformation, or unauthorized transactions.

The hiring of financial personnel needs to be considered in the light of professional duties. Emphasis on specialization of finance personnel means that a financial manager has access to new, highly specialized personnel, but they need to fit into the organization's culture objectives, particularly with respect to risk management attitudes.

Financial Institution and Vendor Relationships

Maintenance of good relationships with financial institutions and other vendors is important. Good relationships with an appropriate number of financial institutions or dealers, with at least one backup, should be maintained. Overreliance on, or a majority of transactions with, one institution or individual representative should be questioned.

Relationship maintenance includes ensuring that correct documentation is provided when a new employee joins who is responsible for transactions. A list of authorized dealing personnel should be provided to counterparties on at least an annual basis and whenever a change occurs. Financial institutions should be informed in writing when key employees have left the organization. This helps to avoid opportunities for errors, embarrassment, or intentional misrepresentation.

Monitoring Exposures

An important operational activity is to monitor exposures. It is important to keep up to date with market or regulatory changes that might affect a currency's convertibility or liquidity, especially for emerging-market currencies.

In addition, maintain an understanding of counterparty issues and monitor counterparty viability, as well as agency ratings. Exposure to high-quality counterparties is preferable, though not a guarantee of loss prevention.

Organizations using exchange-traded contracts such as futures must ensure that margin can be administered by someone else, in the event of a margin call, if key personnel are unavailable.

Exposure assessment is discussed in more detail in Chapter 9.

Communication and Reporting

Appropriate and adequate reporting to team, management, and the board is important, as is a feedback loop that enables report recipients to ask questions and offer suggestions for improvement. Reporting should include both exposures and risk management activities.

Reporting and communications mechanisms should ensure that management and the board receives regular risk reports containing communication about risk exceptions, deviations from policy, reports about deficiencies, unusual losses, or anything else that would permit management and the board to better assess exposures and risk.

Reporting should be adequate to ensure adherence to risk management policies and limits and deviation from policy. Information should be available based on different criteria and detail, although this, in part, depends on the systems being used to produce the reports.

Forecasts and Reconciliations

Cash forecasts have a variety of purposes. First and foremost, they are used to manage an organization's liquidity and obligations. Forecasts and reconciliation of actual transactions to forecasted transactions also assist in the important identification of errors and certain fraudulent items.

From a risk management perspective, cash forecasts should be developed and maintained for the various currencies in which an organization has cash flows. A gap or mismatch between cash inflows and cash outflows for a particular currency provides information about gaps where funding is required or to assess foreign currency exposure. A forecast will assist in determining whether a gap is a timing issue or an exposure issue.

Not only does a cash forecast assist in highlighting areas of market exposure, but it also assists in liquidity management. Liquidity management ensures that an organization is adequately solvent to meet its immediate and short-term obligations. Reminder systems or other automated tools should be used to ensure that cashflows are properly anticipated and that key payment dates are met. Other date-sensitive issues, such as option expiry dates, should also be tracked closely.

Reconciliations should include analysis of brokerage fees or commissions that may provide clues about trading volumes or unauthorized trading.

Risk Oversight

Typically, treasury activities are overseen by one or more members of senior management, and ultimately, by the board of directors. The board should have a good understanding of the financial risks faced by the firm, provide leadership in the development of policies to measure and manage those risks, and ensure that management executes the plans quickly and effectively. The risk oversight function should be an independent function with reporting responsibility to top-level senior management and the board of directors, with a level of skills appropriate to the position. Issues of risk policy, including risk oversight, are discussed in Chapter 8.

Marking to Market

Marking to market involves repricing financial instruments, and sometimes the underlying exposures the instruments manage. It is an important risk management process. Large accumulated gains and losses should be monitored and assessed for potential follow-up action.

When marking to market, it is important to include all determinants of market value. For example, certain derivative products might be difficult to liquidate quickly, and a liquidity impact (premium or discount) may be appropriate. Nontraded transactions with a counterparty whose credit quality has declined substantially since the transaction was initiated might also require a pricing assessment of liquidity.

Marking to market should include the use of industry-standard pricing models. One reason for access to pricing models is to ensure that the organization is receiving competitive pricing on its transactions.

Pricing models should be documented and periodically evaluated against an external source, so that discrepancies between those used internally and those used by external market participants can be determined. It is also useful to check that internal mark-to-market prices would be comparable to those calculated using the documented pricing models. If pricing can be manipulated internally, it increases opportunity for loss.

Exchange-traded financial instruments can be valued using a real-time data vendor, since these instruments are standardized, and market prices for various contracts may be observed directly. Prices for actively traded money market and fixed income securities, and some over-the-counter derivatives, can also be found on several major data vendors.

Periodic pricing or mark-to-market should be undertaken by individuals other than the traders involved in the transactions, preferably from within the risk oversight or management function. This may require individuals other than those executing transactions to become familiar with, and have access to, pricing software and real-time data. Prices should not be supplied by those responsible for undertaking the transactions (e.g., traders).

Policies

Management and board members require an understanding of risks for the development of policies. Stated policies on financial risk, exposures, and limits assist in the management of financial risk. Policies should include acceptable instruments and strategies. Limits should encompass the amount of exposure the firm has defined as acceptable risk and loss limits associated with it, and the limits on various types of transactions.

Policy issues include:

- Existence of policies

- Adherence to policies

- Periodic review of policies

Policies are developed by management, and significant policies are approved and reviewed by the board. Policies should be periodically reviewed for any necessary changes or updates. Management should be capable of ensuring adherence to risk management policy through oversight and reporting.

System Considerations

Operational risk arises from technology and systems. Managing this risk often involves control of access to networks and trading systems, particularly third-party systems that support both real-time data and transactions, control of access to locations where technology or networks can be accessed, and employee use of hard-to-break passwords and log-in/log-out rules. Data should be protected through onsite and offsite data backups, with availability of a remote location in the event of a physical evacuation.

The ability to conduct transactions from real-time vendor systems is a source of exposure. Often these systems are presumed by management to be interactive price retrieval data systems, but some permit messaging and trading. Therefore, they should not be accessible by disgruntled former employees or unauthorized individuals such as consultants, visitors, or other employees. Internal and external systems should support multiple access and authority levels. Some employees may be permitted to change or modify records, others can enter new records, and some employees can only read records. Reports should be protected against an employee modifying report parameters, such as those used for exception reports, through the use of report-writing tools. The integration of systems or software to manage cashflows, market risk, and credit risk is useful.

Spreadsheets are widely used in both financial and nonfinancial organizations, but reliance on them, combined with lack of controls, can create operational exposure. Significant losses have resulted from erroneous calculations contained in spreadsheets. Creating an inventory of spreadsheets and their uses, complexity, and potential for error or misuse may help to highlight areas of risk.

Systems should provide timeliness, accuracy, security and integrity, consistency, completeness, and relevance in the provision of data to the organization and its stakeholders. As technology is a fairly complex area, the guidance of professionals in this area is highly recommended.

Professional Assistance

Professional assistance on a variety of financial risk management topics is available from many sources. Financial institutions are able to discuss the characteristics of products and the strategies for using them. As vendors of such products, their intention is usually to match their customers' needs with appropriate hedging products. Since they sell products, their perspective is naturally biased toward those products.

TIPS & TECHNIQUES

Exchange Resources

Exchanges spend significant resources in the education of financial market participants, offering educational materials, courses, and seminars for market participants. Generally, these resources involve listed derivatives and how they are used for hedging or trading. Information specific to the contracts they offer, as well as primers on product mechanics and hedging, can be helpful in understanding the basics of a specific market.

Many consulting firms have practices in risk management, due mainly to strength gained in other areas such as in corporate finance. Consulting firms offer highly skilled professionals in a number of areas who are available on a contractual or project basis. These are most often reached through referrals from other professionals. It is important to ensure which professionals will be working on a particular project and whether the firm is also a provider or vendor of risk management products such as technology.

Risk management associations and organizations provide education, and in some cases certification, ranging from introductory to highly specific. Some of these organizations are listed in the Appendix.

A small number of independent firms manage functions such as currency and interest rate risk on behalf of clients. These overlay managers are compensated in the form of fees. Money managers also use outsourcing when there is insufficient staff expertise to manage specialized risks.

Special Issues in Managing Operational Risk

Trading and Leverage

Special risks exist in organizations where trading, with or without the use of leverage, is involved. Since trading organizations such as dealers and commercial banks use large numbers of dealers and capital, the risks are naturally greater for an operational failure. It is critical to manage these risks proactively.

Trading can be purely speculative, or it can be a form of trading that optimizes business flows. The nature of trading is similar to a continuum, with pure trading at one end and complete hedging at the other end. An organization's position on the continuum depends to a certain degree on the organizational view of risk versus return. These topics are discussed in more detail in Chapter 8.

IN THE REAL WORLD

Notable Quote

"Of the series of great derivatives disasters in the middle of the 1990s, only one, that of Metallgesellschaft (loss $1.5 billion), has been caused by the mishandling of bona fide hedging transactions.

"The others—Barings (loss £850 million), Orange County (loss $1.7 billion), and Sumitomo (loss $2.6 billion)—have been the result of unhedged and unauthorized speculation."

Source: Edward Chancellor, writing in *Devil Take the Hindmost* (New York: Plume Publishing, 1999), pp. 248–249. Copyright Edward Chancellor.

Merger and Acquisitions

Merger and acquisition situations present specific operational risks that need to be managed, not only during the often-lengthy transition phase but also after the transition is completed. The additional risks arise from the fact that it is more difficult to manage risk across an organization that might be geographically distant and involve various systems. In addition, different business cultures and practices may need to be taken into account, along with potentially different legal and regulatory environments.

Centralization

Many large multinational corporations and financial institutions have centralized trading, risk management, or treasury operations. These operations manage regional, or in some cases worldwide, exposures by netting hedging and liquidity requirements among members of the group.

Centralization has certain advantages, including the potential to reduce transaction costs associated with hedging. It may allow smaller group members access to skilled professionals in the operational center. However, the biggest consideration in centralization is risk, which arises through reduced control in key operational areas and through more reliance on reporting and quantitative measures. Strong operational controls and effective reporting become particularly important in centralized organizations.

Industry Recommendations

Group of 31: Core Principles

The Group of 31: Core Principles for Managing Multinational Financial Exchange Risk arose from a 1998 study of foreign exchange risk management multinational corporations sponsored by General Motors and undertaken by Greenwich Treasury Advisors LLC.[i] The study surveyed 31 large multinational corporations with foreign exchange exposure arising from business activities—13 American, 2 Japanese, and 13 European companies with average sales of U.S.$50 billion. A follow-up study looked at the activities of an additional 33 U.S. multinational corporations with average sales of U.S.$11 billion.

Twelve core principles for managing foreign exchange exposure were used by a majority of firms. The core principles include fundamental principles, trading-volume-related principles, and principles related to risk-appetite.

Although they specifically reflect foreign exchange exposure management, the principles may also be helpful in the management of other financial risks.

Fundamental Principles

1. *Document foreign exchange policy.* Document a foreign exchange policy approved by senior management or the board of directors. Critical policy elements include hedging objectives, hedgeable exposures, hedging time horizon, authorized foreign exchange derivatives, the extent to which positions can be managed upon views of future foreign exchange rates, compensation for foreign exchange trader performance, and hedging performance measures.

2. *Hire well-qualified, experienced personnel.* Have a sufficient number of qualified, experienced personnel to properly execute the company's foreign exchange policy.

3. *Centralize foreign exchange trading and risk management.* Centralize the foreign exchange trading and risk management with the parent treasury, which may be assisted by foreign hedging centers reporting to parent treasury.

4. *Adopt uniform foreign exchange accounting procedures.* Require uniform foreign exchange accounting procedures, uniform exchange rates for book purposes, and multicurrency general ledgers for all foreign exchange transactions. Monthly, reconcile the parent treasury's foreign exchange hedging results to the group's consolidated generally accepted accounting principles (GAAP) foreign exchange results.

5. *Manage foreign exchange forecast error.* If anticipated foreign exchange exposures are being hedged, manage the forecast error and take steps to minimize it to the greatest extent possible.

6. *Measure hedging performance.* Use several performance measures to fully evaluate historic hedging effectiveness. Evaluate current hedging performance by frequently marking to market both the outstanding hedges and the underlying exposures.

Trading-Volume-Related Principles

7. *Segregate the back office function.* Segregate back office operations such as confirmations and settlements from trading. If trading volume is sufficient, use nostro accounts and net settle.

8. *Manage counterparty risk.* Have credit rating standards and evaluate counterparty risk at least quarterly. Measure credit exposure using market valuations, not notional amounts, against assigned counterparty credit limits. Use ISDA or other kinds of master agreements with at least major counterparties.

9. *Buy derivatives competitively.* Execute the foreign exchange policy by competitively buying foreign exchange derivatives with appropriate trading controls.

Risk-Appetite-Related Principles

10. *Use pricing models and systems.* Have in-house pricing models for all derivatives used. Use automated systems to track, manage, and value the derivatives traded and the underlying business exposures being hedged.

11. *Measure foreign exchange risk.* Understand the full nature of the foreign exchange risks being managed with a combination of risk measures such as value-at-risk, sensitivity analysis, and stress testing.

12. *Oversee treasury's risk management.* Independently oversee treasury's risk management with a risk committee to review and approve treasury's risk-taking activities and strategies, exposure and counterparty credit limits, and exceptions to corporate foreign exchange policy. Depending on the level of foreign exchange risks being managed, have either a part-time or a dedicated function to review treasury's compliance with approved risk management policies and procedures.

Group of 30 Recommendations[ii]

A seminal report by the *Group of 30* more than a decade ago addressed how both dealers and end-user organizations could better control the risks associated with the use of derivatives. It remains a classic set of fundamental risk management principles and may be useful to decision makers involved in risk management. The relevant recommendations of the Group of 30 are:

1. *The role of senior management.* Dealers and end users should use derivatives in a manner consistent with the overall risk management and capital policies approved by their boards of directors. These policies should be reviewed as business and market circumstances change. Policies governing derivatives use should be clearly defined, including the purposes for which these transactions are to be undertaken. Senior management should approve procedures and controls to implement these policies, and management at all levels should enforce them.

2. *Marking to market.* Dealers should mark their derivatives positions to market, on at least a daily basis, for risk management purposes.

3. *Market valuation methods.* Derivatives portfolios of dealers should be valued based on mid-market levels less specific adjustments, or on appropriate bid or offer levels. Mid-market valuation adjustments should allow for expected future costs such as unearned credit spread, close-out costs, investing and funding costs, and administrative costs.

4. *Identifying revenue sources.* Dealers should measure the components of revenue regularly and in sufficient detail to understand the sources of risk.

5. *Measuring market risk.* Dealers should use a consistent measure to calculate daily the market risk of their derivatives positions and compare it to market risk limits.

- Market risk is best measured as *value at risk* using probability analysis based on a common confidence interval (e.g., two standard deviations) and time horizon (e.g., a one-day exposure).

- Components of market risk that should be considered across the term structure include absolute price or rate change (delta); convexity (gamma); volatility (vega); time decay (theta); basis or correlation; and discount rate (rho).

6. *Stress simulations.* Dealers should regularly perform simulations to determine how their portfolios would perform under stress conditions.

7. *Investing and funding forecasts.* Dealers should periodically forecast the cash investing and funding requirements arising from their derivatives portfolios.

8. *Independent market risk management.* Dealers should have a market risk management function, with clear independence and authority, to ensure that the following responsibilities are carried out:

- Development of risk limit policies and monitoring of transactions and positions for adherence to these policies (See recommendation 5.)

- Design of stress scenarios to measure the impact of market conditions, however improbable, that might cause market gaps, volatility swings, or disruptions of major relationships, or might reduce liquidity in the face of unfavorable market linkages, concentrated market making, or credit exhaustion (See recommendation 6.)

- Design of revenue reports quantifying the contribution of various risk components, and of market risk measures such as the value at risk (See recommendations 4 and 5.)

- Monitoring of variance between the actual volatility of portfolio value and that predicted by the measure of market risk

- Review and approval of pricing models and valuation systems used by front- and back-office personnel, and the development of reconciliation procedures if different systems are used

9. *Practices by end users.* As appropriate to the nature, size, and complexity of their derivatives activities, end users should adopt the same valuation and market risk management practices that are recommended for dealers. Specifically, they should consider regularly marking to market their derivatives transactions for risk management purposes; periodically forecasting the cash investing and funding requirements arising from their derivatives transactions; and establishing a clearly independent and authoritative function to design and assure adherence to prudent risk limits.

10. *Measuring credit exposure.* Dealers and end users should measure credit exposure on derivatives in two ways:

- *Current exposure* is the replacement cost of derivatives trans-actions—that is, their market value.

- *Potential exposure* is an estimate of the future replacement cost of derivatives transactions. It should be calculated using probability analysis based on broad confidence inter-vals (e.g., two standard deviations) over the remaining terms of the transactions.

11. *Aggregating credit exposures.* Credit exposures on derivatives, and all other credit exposures to a counterparty, should be aggregated taking into consideration enforceable netting arrangements. Credit exposures should be calculated regularly and compared to credit limits.

12. *Independent credit risk management.* Dealers and end users should have a credit risk management function with clear independence and authority, and with analytical capabilities in derivatives, responsible for the following:

- Approving credit exposure measurement standards

- Setting credit limits and monitoring their use

- Reviewing credits and concentrations of credit risk

- Reviewing and monitoring risk reduction arrangements

13. *Master agreements.* Dealers and end users are encouraged to use one master agreement as widely as possible with each counterparty to document existing and future derivatives transactions, including foreign exchange forwards and options. Master agreements should provide for payments netting and closes out netting, using a full two-way payments approach.

14. *Credit enhancement.* Dealers and end users should assess both the benefits and costs of credit enhancement and related risk–reduction arrangements. Where it is proposed that credit downgrades would trigger early termination or collateral requirements, participants should carefully consider their own capacity and that of their counterparties to meet the potentially substantial funding needs that might result.

15. *Promoting enforceability.* Dealers and end users should work together on a continuing basis to identify and recommend solutions for issues of legal enforceability, both within and across jurisdictions, as activities evolve and new types of transactions are developed.

16. *Professional expertise.* Dealers and end users must ensure that their derivatives activities are undertaken by professionals in sufficient number and with the appropriate experience, skill levels, and degrees of specialization. These professionals include specialists who transact and manage the risks involved, their supervisors, and those responsible for processing, reporting, controlling, and auditing the activities.

17. *Systems.* Dealers and end users must ensure that adequate systems for data capture, processing, settlement, and management reporting are in place so that derivatives transactions are conducted in an orderly and efficient manner in compliance with management policies. Dealers should have risk management systems that measure the risks incurred in their derivatives activities, including market and credit risks. End users should have risk management systems that measure the risks incurred in their derivatives activities based on their nature, size, and complexity.

18. *Authority*. Management of dealers and end users should designate who is authorized to commit their institutions to derivatives transactions.

19. *Accounting practices*. International harmonization of accounting standards for derivatives is desirable. Pending the adoption of harmonized standards, the following accounting policies are recommended:

- Dealers should account for derivatives transactions by marking them to market, taking changes in value to income each period.

- End users should account for derivatives used to manage risks so as to achieve a consistency of income recognition treatment between those instruments and the risks being managed. Thus, if the risk being managed is accounted for at cost (or, in the case of an anticipatory hedge, not yet recognized), changes in the value of a qualifying risk management instrument should be deferred until a gain or loss is recognized on the risk being managed. Or, if the risk being managed is marked to market with changes in value being taken to income, a qualifying risk management instrument should be treated in a comparable fashion.

- End users should account for derivatives not qualifying for risk management treatment on a mark-to-market basis.

- Amounts due to and from counterparties should only be offset when there is a legal right to set off or when enforceable netting arrangements are in place.

Where local regulations prevent adoption of these practices, disclosure along these lines is nevertheless recommended.

20. *Disclosures*. Financial statements of dealers and end users should contain sufficient information about their use of derivatives to provide an understanding of the purposes for which transactions are undertaken, the extent of the transactions, the degree of risk involved, and how the transactions have been accounted for. Pending the adoption of harmonized accounting standards, the following disclosures are recommended:

- Information about management's attitude to financial risks, how instruments are used, and how risks are monitored and controlled

- Accounting policies

- Analysis of positions at the balance sheet date

- Analysis of the credit risk inherent in those positions

- For dealers only, additional information about the extent of their activities in financial instruments

Summary

- Operational risk arises from the possibility of error, fraud, or a gap in procedures or systems. It is one of the most prevalent risks that organizations face.

- Operational risks are exacerbated in situations where additional risks exist, such as during mergers or acquisitions, trading environments, or geographically diverse organizations.

- Management of people, processes such as reporting and controls, and an assessment of the technological risks an organization faces may be useful in identifying and managing operational risk.

Notes

i *Group of 31: Core Principles for Managing Multinational Financial Exchange Risk,* The Group of 31/Greenwich Treasury Advisors LLC. Copyright 1999 by Greenwich Treasury Advisors LLC. Reproduced with permission.

ii *Group of 30 Global Derivatives Study Group; Derivatives: Practices and Principles,* Washington, DC, July 1993. Copyright protected. Reproduced with permission.

CHAPTER 8

Risk Management Framework: Policy and Hedging

After reading this chapter you will be able to

- Comment on the importance of financial risk management policy
- Develop an organizational profile to support risk management policy
- Evaluate opportunities to develop or refine a risk management policy

Financial risk management addresses factors that concern many organizations. In addition to general business risks, other factors include exposure to market prices, tolerance for risk, an organization's history, and its stakeholders. Assessing these issues for risk management purposes may facilitate useful discussion among decision makers that provides benefits in other areas.

The risk management policy is a framework that allows an organization to grow by building decision-making processes instead of treating each decision independently. The policy is a tool for communicating what constitutes an acceptable level of risk to individuals throughout an organization. The procedures that arise from the development of a policy may support performance indicators, incentives for management, and efficiency. Finally, a risk management policy supports the organization's market views and risk appetite. Over time, it can incorporate changes based on growth or recent events.

The risk management policy supports financial risk management and its questions:

- How are we at risk?

- What is an acceptable level of risk?

- How much will it cost to manage risk?

- What are our risk management policies?

- How do we manage risk within our policies?

- How do we communicate information in a timely and accurate manner?

Although publicly traded companies in many countries have increased requirements to establish policies and procedures to manage risk, all organizations should develop risk management policies to identify and manage risks that reflect their business and industry. The alternative, to do nothing, is to accept all risks by default.

Risk Profile of an Organization

The development of a risk management policy requires an understanding of the organization's risk profile. The risk profile depends, in turn, on attributes such as risk tolerance, financial position within the industry, management culture, stakeholders, and the competitive landscape in which it operates. The risk profile of an organization is unique. The combination of an organization's business, products, and people makes each organization's exposure to risk slightly different.

These attributes will be explored in more detail, but they include:

- Specific exposures that impact an organization

- Market in which an organization operates

- Risk tolerance of the organization

- Management, stakeholders, and the board

Once risks and exposures have been identified, they can be assessed and prioritized.

Evaluating Financial Exposures

The first step in managing financial risk is to identify the relevant exposures. Since broad risks are often composed of a number of different risks, such as price risk, liquidity risk, and volatility risk, all should be considered for their potential impact on the business. For example, it is important to be able to separate market risk from credit risk and liquidity risk.

Not all exposures are obvious. A business with foreign currency revenues may have both transaction exposure and economic exposure. If the foreign currency declines against the domestic currency, its revenues (once converted to the domestic currency) will have declined. However, foreign revenues may also decline, since the appreciation of the domestic currency may make the organization's products expensive and therefore uncompetitive.

To Hedge or Not to Hedge

Whether to hedge or not to hedge is a strategic decision. Although most larger organizations use an explicit hedging policy, some do not. The determination of what and how much to hedge depends to a degree on the business, reliability of forecasts, and management's assessment of various exposures.

Without hedging, an organization may be exposed to unfavorable as well as favorable market rate and price changes. Although providing

Evaluating Risk
in a New Currency

A company is considering selling to a new customer in an emerging market. Evaluation of the potential foreign exchange risk might include examining the qualitative features of the currency itself, such as:

- Is it a major industrial or emerging market currency?

- Is it a freely traded currency with both purchases and sales permitted?

- Does the currency exchange rate operate under a pegged or target rate regime?

- Can funds be freely moved into or out of the country?

- Are forwards and options available for hedging purposes?

- Can the business alternatively be conducted in a major currency such as U.S. dollars or euros?

- Can the company's domestic financial institution handle the payments and exchange? If not, what are their comments about doing business in the country?

- What is the underlying legal system?

- Are any aspects of ordinary financial transactions limited, or do the transactions otherwise require special permission, fees, or paperwork by the sovereign government?

- Is there any sign of civil, political, or social unrest that could potentially result in financial crisis?

- Does market intelligence from operations or contacts in the region, industry, or within the organization suggest a cautionary approach?

an opportunity to increase profits, it also provides opportunity for losses. Hedging may make it easier to budget and allocate organizational resources efficiently.

Tolerance for Risk

Risk management involves reducing the probability of loss. Determining an acceptable level of risk and exposure then guides risk management strategies. Decisions about how much loss can be tolerated are important organizational guidelines.

Risk tolerance is the ability or willingness to withstand risk. It depends on the culture of an organization, which in turn is shaped by its shareholders or stakeholders, management's relationship with them, and their understanding of the risks.

The determination of an acceptable level of risk is important, since business and risk are interconnected. Therefore, the risk tolerance decision involves determining a reasonable level of risk commensurate with appropriate opportunity for profit or gain.

Management, shareholders, and employees of large and small companies, privately held and publicly traded corporations, financial institutions, investment funds, domestic and international governments, and not-for-profit organizations all have a stake in risk management.

The risk tolerance of an organization depends on fundamental cultural issues, as well as the nature of the business and industry. In developing a hedging policy, it may be helpful to consider the following issues:

- *The structure of an organization may provide clues about its risk tolerance.* In a closely held company, for example, a majority of shareholders might be management and founders' families. With a small number of stakeholders, risk tolerance may be higher because information flows more easily and provides

TIPS & TECHNIQUES

Risk Tolerance

It is inappropriate to categorize an organization's risk tolerance on simplistic measures such as annual revenues or number of employees. Instead, the risk tolerance of an organization is better assessed by an understanding of the organization's culture.

stakeholders with more assurance. However, family companies may also exhibit dynamics that adversely affect financial risk tolerance, particularly if some family members have a greater understanding of, or interest in, the subject, than others.

- *The business of the organization may provide guidance in risk tolerance.* Financial institutions, for example, are typically (though not always) more conversant with financial risks. Major market risks such as interest rate risk and credit risk are key components of the business of a financial institution. Companies with a trading history may also have a higher tolerance for risk than other organizations.

- *The origins of the business may impact organizational culture for decades.* For example, some commodities trading houses have been in the trading business longer than some countries have been in existence. If the founders took great risks in achieving success, or if they have a background in speculation, risk tolerance may be strongly impacted (positively or negatively) as a result.

- *The characteristics of the stakeholders should be considered.* In publicly traded companies, the stakeholders—including employees and shareholders—can walk away if they do not like the risks the company is taking on. By contrast, stakeholders of government, or even charitable, organizations do not generally have the ability to opt out. In addition, they may have little or no understanding of the financial risks of the organization and little tolerance for paying a higher price for services (or receiving fewer services in the case of a charitable organization). Risk tolerance may therefore be lower in such organizations.

Acceptable Risk Exposure

It is easy to focus on common risks, or on events that have occurred in recent history, at the expense of events that occur infrequently but have major impact. Significant risks are those that are material to an organization. Materiality varies by organization.

Consider these questions when assessing and quantifying acceptable loss:

- What is a material individual loss?

- What are the aggregate acceptable losses over a period of time such as one year?

- What is the maximum amount that the organization can afford to lose?

- Can the organization reduce the potential impact of a maximum loss scenario?

Risks are events and described as high or low probability. If an event occurs, it has the potential for losses that range in size from small to large. Often, one measure is high and the other is low—for example, a high probability of a small loss. This type of loss might be represented by routine exchange rate fluctuations.

The most dangerous risks are those with a low probability of occurring but the potential for a large loss. Sometimes known as *icebergs,* these risks appear suddenly and can result in large losses. The failure of a counterparty and the resultant loss could be an example of such a risk.

Once an acceptable level of exposure has been established, management can determine how to reduce the potential for loss to an acceptable level.

Competitive Landscape

An important consideration in making hedging decisions is the expected activity of competitors. If an organization hedges and its major competitors do not, the organization may be at a disadvantage if market rates or prices move favorably. The reverse is also true. If the organization hedges and exchange rates move adversely, the organization may have an advantage over its competitors.

Changes to an organization's pricing structure, as a result of changing costs, may cause customers to buy or consume more or less. Financial risk can sometimes be passed on to customers or end users in the form of price adjustments, reducing the impact to the organization. This is most often possible when demand is inflexible or slow to react to price changes.

The activities of competitors and the market affect the competitive landscape in the following ways:

- Propensity of customers to accept risk through rising prices

- Willingness of vendors to offer fixed-price contracts or dual-currency pricing

- How products are priced

- Where product inputs, including commodity components, are sourced

- Alternative inputs to products and sources of inputs

- Commodity components

Board and Management: Role, Requirements, and Challenges

Management typically develops risk management policy, while the board of directors has responsibility for its approval. As representatives of shareholders, the board's responsibilities include oversight of management. Given the potential for substantial losses, boards are especially concerned about financial risk management and its implications in these key areas:

- Policy

- Strategy

- Oversight

Management and the board play a vital role in the development of an appropriate risk management policy. An organization can then develop strategies that are acceptable and consistent with policy. The policy is intended for use by management and staff in their duties. If one does not exist, staff should insist on its development.

In order to make decisions and guide an organization, both the board of directors and management have specific informational requirements with differing needs for detail. Both groups require information that is:

- Reliable

- Timely

- Accessible

- Accurate

- Consistent in format

- Suited to different users

With increasingly complex financial products, the board and senior management must be capable of understanding implications of prospective changes to policy or strategy. Some challenges can be addressed through appropriate education, reporting, and oversight. Members of management and the board must understand the following:

- The financial risks being taken by the organization in the course of business

- Planned financial instruments and strategies for managing financial risks

- Risks of any unusual financial instruments or strategies

- Risk measurement methodologies and their relationship to policy

- Understanding of financial risk reporting results

- Implications of acceptable exposure, risk, or loss limits

- Recognition that it might not be possible to quantify potential losses with certainty

Risk Management Policy

The risk management policy is a critical component of the risk management function. The policy provides and formalizes a framework for making individual decisions and reflects the organization's perspective on risk. The risk management policy is predicated on setting organizational priorities, which are discussed in the first half of this chapter.

The risk management policy can be as broad as the risks facing an organization and may include disaster planning, investment policy, and insurance, the traditional arena of risk management. This discussion will focus on the financial risk management policy, comprising market, credit, and operational exposures.

Developed by management and approved by the board, the policy should be reviewed and updated as often as necessary to maintain its

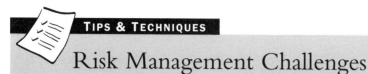

TIPS & TECHNIQUES

Risk Management Challenges

Although some of the challenges that arise in risk management are internally preventable, others arise from the nature of the business or the industry. These challenges include:

- Geographically dispersed reporting entities (e.g., branch plants)

- Different time zones, language, reporting, regulatory environments

- Level of knowledge, experience, interest, or understanding of issues

- Poor or inadequate information, reports, or communications

- Inappropriate delegation of tasks and duties

- Psychological constraints (e.g., "reports are too complex")

- Lack of independence in board of directors

validity as the risks and the organization evolve. Management should be prepared to solicit internal feedback in its development as well as outside or professional help, if necessary.

There are three major reasons for a risk management policy:

- To provide a framework for decision making

- To mandate a policy for controlling risk

- To facilitate measurement and reporting of risk

Each component of the risk management policy is important to its overall success in implementation. The policy should include a clear

Organizational Priorities
for Discussion

Organizations spend significant time and energy producing sales and cashflow forecasts, yet they sometimes fail to formulate priorities and objectives for risk management. This makes it difficult for financial managers who must make decisions without a clear strategic mandate.

The following list addresses issues that organizations may wish to consider when assessing their priorities and the requirements of a financial risk management program:

- What are the major financial risks that threaten the organization? Can those risks be isolated into component parts, such as currency market risk or credit risk? How will the exposures to these risks be measured?

- What is the organization's risk tolerance? Risk tolerance should be reviewed periodically. Financial managers need policies to make appropriate organizational decisions.

- Do senior management, the board of directors, and major shareholders approve of the hedging program? These individuals should be brought into the planning process as early as possible, before strategies are ready for implementation.

- How will major adverse movements beyond the accepted risk tolerance level be managed? What products and strategies are acceptable?

- What is the expected time requirement for financial risk management? The time required by personnel for assessing and determining the correct course of action is often underestimated in planning. Well-informed decisions cannot be made without sufficient time to conduct the necessary analysis.

- What data and information sources are necessary to monitor market activity and keep up to date with changes that could adversely effect the organization? Who is responsible for reporting this information?

- How do major competitors manage their financial risks? An industry leader might maximize market-related opportunities if exchange rates provide an opportunity to increase market share.

- Do finance personnel have the appropriate levels of analytical expertise? Financial risk management involves valuation and modeling under various outcomes and different scenarios.

- What are the accounting and tax requirements for risk management products employed? Is the required treatment of gains and losses from hedging transactions in the financial statements consistent with generally accepted accounting principles or location regulations?

- How will the effectiveness of hedging strategies be measured and monitored?

- Does the organization have access to market prices, or will prices come from the original market maker or trader, which presents potential for conflicts?

- What processes and funds are available to ensure that risk management and treasury staff keep their skills up to date?

- Which financial risks can be managed, and which risks will be accepted by default?

delineation of responsibility for various risk management tasks. Appropriate risk measurement methodologies and acceptable limits for risk tolerance must be determined.

The flow of information from reporting is an integral part of the risk management process, and this should also be addressed by the policy. Management and the board need enough information to determine whether the responsibilities are being handled appropriately, within specified guidelines or parameters. The move toward a single measure for financial risk, such as value-at-risk, is discussed in more detail in Chapter 9.

Limits should be implemented for financial risks, particularly market and credit risk. Activities and objectives of the organization need to be considered in the formulation of limits. Transactional limits might include maximum size of transactions, number of permitted transactions, and counterparty limits. If the organization has an investment management operation, the investment policy will include portfolio and concentration limits.

Risk Oversight

Typically, finance and treasury activities are overseen by senior management, and ultimately, the board of directors with responsibility to the stakeholders. Board members should have a good understanding of the financial risks faced by the organization, provide leadership to ensure the development of policies to measure and manage risks, and ensure that management executes the plans effectively.

An independent risk management function typically reports to senior management—for example, the chief executive officer. There should also be reporting to the board of directors. Individual business departments provide reports to the risk management group. The intent of the risk management role is oversight of, and independence from, the group responsible for executing strategies.

Board, management, and ultimately stakeholders inherit all risks that arise from individual business units, projects, and markets. Resources are needed to support the decisions that are made on their behalf by management and the board. The existence of an independent risk oversight function gives management a level of comfort. It answers the question, "Who is looking after risk management?"

Hedging Policy

A subset of a broad risk management policy deals with financial risks. Known as a hedging policy, or financial risk management policy, it provides clear direction on the organization's approach to managing financial risks. High-level decisions about what and how much to hedge are policy decisions. They are strategic decisions and should involve senior management and the board.

Developing a hedging policy requires knowledgeable input from various groups that are responsible for sources of risk. Knowledgeable

TIPS & TECHNIQUES

Percentage to Hedge

There are no specific rules that determine how much of an organization's exposure is typically hedged. Many organizations hedge one-half to two-thirds of their exposure and some do not hedge at all. The percentage to hedge often depends on the risk culture of the organization, including its risk tolerance. It may also be affected by what is standard in the industry.

input includes an understanding of the financial risks facing the organization and the organization's risk tolerance. With the potential to impact competitive position, the impact of hedging and its opportunity costs should be considered, in addition to an assessment of the cost of risk reduction or mitigation (sometimes referred to as the cost/payoff profile).

Hedging strategies are not designed to anticipate the market. The intent is to reduce or eliminate the risks associated with market fluctuations. It is a fair bet that the future is unlikely to look like the past. As many organizations have discovered, it's easier, and often cheaper, to preemptively hedge than to successfully forecast markets.

Hedging policy helps to avoid judgment by hindsight. Importantly, it provides staff and management with a clear mandate for their daily decisions.

Derivatives

A risk management policy should specify what derivative products are acceptable, and whether an organization is permitted to use forwards, futures, swaps, or options, or a combination of strategies. The policy should specify whether products can be bought or sold, particularly with respect to options and related derivatives.

In addition to the publicity surrounding losses as a result of derivatives usage, lawsuits have resulted when the board of directors of an organization failed to ensure that hedges against market risk were undertaken. Therefore, avoidance of derivatives altogether may not necessarily be an alternative. Where there are concerns about legal responsibilities, it is critical to obtain the advice of professionals.

Potential Components
of Financial Risk Management Policy

The hedging policy should cover the *who, what, when, where,* and *how* of financial risk. It should address market risk management, as well as credit risk and operational risk issues. The policy will usually outline specific limitations with respect to individuals involved in hedging, types of permitted transactions, and other considerations.

Coverage of individuals concerned with hedging might include:

- Who is permitted to enter into trades

- Authority for trade approval

- Responsibility for receipt of trade confirmations

- What constitutes an appropriate division of duties

Coverage of types of transactions might include:

- Types of permitted transactions and strategies

- Dollar limit for individual hedge transactions

- Dollar limit for hedge transactions in total

- Maximum time to maturity/expiry for individual transactions

- Whether both sale and purchase of derivatives are permitted

Coverage of other policy considerations might include:

- Under what conditions hedges can be unwound once they are in place

continued on next page

TIPS & TECHNIQUES CONTINUED

- Minimum credit quality of hedge counterparties and debt issuers

- Action required when a counterparty's credit quality deteriorates

- Dollar or percentage limit on transactions with one counterparty

- Benchmark percentage to hedge

- Number of price quotes to obtain before undertaking large transactions

- Restrictions on open orders (e.g., overnight) and positions

Hedging Strategy Selection

Hedging decisions always involve a trade-off between an appropriate level of risk and opportunities for gain. Every strategy has a price, whether it is the explicit cost of hedging products or the opportunity cost arising from being hedged.

Hedging strategy should be in alignment with an organization's business objectives. Hedging products should be chosen for their effectiveness in risk management from the universe of acceptable products and strategies. The hedging decision should be based on business objectives and tolerance for risk, rather than on market conditions.

The risk profiles of options and forwards (or futures) differ. Forwards effectively offset price risk, although they do not eliminate basis risk. If guaranteeing a particular rate is very important, or if individual transactions are large, an organization may choose to reduce or eliminate market risk with a forward contract.

IN THE REAL WORLD

Notable Quote

Not everyone is a fan of the increased volumes and types of derivatives. Warren Buffett, chairman of Berkshire Hathaway and one of history's most successful investors, expressed an alternative viewpoint:

"The derivatives genie is now well out of the bottle, and these instruments will almost certainly multiply in variety and number until some event makes their toxicity clear."

Source: Warren Buffett, writing in his in 2002 letter to Berkshire Hathaway shareholders.

Option buyers pay premium for insurance against adverse movements and the ability to gain from favorable movements in interest rates. Option premium depends on a number of factors, including volatility, which greatly influences its price. As a result, options are most expensive at the time that they are most desirable to hedgers.

Provided that it is acceptable policy, a purchased option is sometimes used to enhance the payoff of a profitable forward by locking in a gain on a forward contract to take advantage of subsequent favorable movements. This is a move along the continuum away from pure hedging, since it involves optimizing market opportunities (gains on an existing hedge).

The decision to hedge using forwards or options, or a combination of the two, depends on a number of factors, including the skills and time availability of the financial manager, organizational understanding and acceptance of derivative products, funds available for hedging purposes, the characteristics of the market being hedged, the type of exposure, and the expectation of future market rates.

IN THE REAL WORLD

Where Does Hedging End and Speculation Begin?

Board Member: "With these major moves, I'm glad we set our policy to hedge 65 percent of requirements. That turns out to have been a good decision."

Management: "Well, I know treasury took profits on many of the hedges about a month ago before the last big move really started. Our treasury manager is still on vacation and won't be back until next week. I don't know how much we're actually hedged at the moment."

This fictional conversation between a board member and management illustrates a potential hazard in the definition of hedging, as well as operational failings. A textbook definition of hedging is straightforward, but in reality, it is sometimes difficult to define where hedging ends and speculation begins.

The hedging-speculation distinction is similar to a continuum, with pure hedging at one end and pure speculation at the other. Between the two are variants that might include optimizing market conditions or taking profit on existing hedges. Such activities can potentially leave an organization underhedged or overhedged. Therefore, permissible strategies should be outlined clearly in policy and understood by management and the board, since they provide opportunities for additional, and often unexpected, losses.

A few considerations in hedging products and their uses follow:

- *Forwards (including futures) may eliminate the price risk associated with an exposure, presuming the underlying exposure and product are identical and there is no basis risk.* No explicit costs are typically involved with forwards, although futures involve transaction fees and margin requirements.

- *The buyer of an option obtains protection against adverse changes but retains the ability to gain from favorable changes.* Option premium is the cost to obtain this protection.

- *The seller of an option earns option premium but accepts all obligations associated with the option.* The strategy is more risky because no hedge has been implemented.

- *Swaps permit organizations to change the payment structure of an asset or liability.* As with forwards, exiting from an outstanding swap requires exchanging or netting the net present value of remaining obligations under the swap agreement.

- *Daily price limits are imposed by some futures exchanges.* These limits may prevent the futures price from immediately reflecting changes in the underlying market that is being hedged. See Chapter 6 for more information on price limits.

- *Objectives and expectations help determine strategies.* Forwards typically offset price risk (though not basis risk) and potential gains. Purchased options provide protection and participation in favorable moves. In a significant adverse move, forwards will track the underlying closely, while an option may not, depending on the relationship of its strike price to current market prices.

- *Credit facilities are required for forwards transacted with a financial institution, while futures require only margin.* Purchased options may or may not require credit facilities or margin (it varies, depending on the institution), but sold options require credit facilities in the over-the-counter market or margin if sold through an exchange.

- *Purchased options can provide disaster insurance, or protection, when a market rate moves significantly beyond a comfort level.* Such a hedge may provide a temporary respite from current market rates. The purchased option will provide protection for the notional amount of the contract, with a finite expiry.

TIPS & TECHNIQUES

A Review of Risk Mitigation Approaches

Recall from Chapter 1 that there are three broad alternatives in managing risk:

1. Do nothing and actively, or passively by default, accept all risks.

2. Hedge a portion of exposures by determining which exposures can and should be hedged.

3. Hedge all exposures possible.

Once the alternatives have been assessed, there are two major approaches to hedging, used separately or in combination. The first involves minimizing exposure through opportunistically rearranging business activities. Although this can be time consuming, it may provide long-term benefits including business diversification. The second approach involves the use of derivatives such as forwards, futures, swaps, and options to reduce risk by offsetting exposures where possible.

Risk Measurement

If financial instruments are used to hedge exposures, there should be a focus not on whether profit has been gained but on the extent of the completeness and adequacy of the hedging. Periodic marking to market of net exposures will provide the ability to measure net exposures (actual exposure less any hedging undertaken to reduce exposure), which is more relevant in corporate hedging with financial instruments.

Measurement is a key aspect of policy and risk management. Risk measurement provides an estimation of potential losses. Unfortunately, potential losses cannot be quantified with certainty—losses can only be quantified with certainty once they are realized.

Many organizations use a value-at-risk or similar composite number as a single, all-encompassing measure of risk. The intent of such a composite is to provide management and the board with adequate information and to improve decision making. However, there are weaknesses with such an approach that should be understood by management, the board, and decision makers. Some of these topics are discussed in more detail in Chapter 9.

Reporting

Management reports should provide clear information to senior management and the board of directors. In addition, it should be ensured that users understand the reports they receive. Where there is a lack of understanding, it should be addressed and reports adjusted accordingly to clarify, not simplify. Feedback and augmentation on reports, if necessary, will ensure they address the users' needs. In addition to marking the exposures to market, reports should provide alternative risk measures that allow the readers to understand the potential risks to the organization.

Risk Management Topics for Discussion

The following topics may provide some direction for facilitating discussion about risk management:

- What technology is available for monitoring the effectiveness of hedges and the exposures they manage? Can the organization conduct scenario analysis based on combined exposures and hedges? Can current market prices be determined for exposures and hedges?

- How frequently are cash-flow forecasts updated and reported?

- Are there written policies for individual duties and responsibilities? Is there an appropriate segregation of duties? In smaller organizations, senior management's involvement may help to fulfill division of duty requirements.

- What arrangements exist if staff are unavailable as a result of emergency or unexpected events?

- What reporting does senior management require about exposures and hedging? Management and the board require frequent, accurate reporting about activities and adherence to policy. Can management quickly and easily ascertain the organization's overall position in the case of an unexpected event or crisis?

- For exchange-traded derivatives, who has responsibility for reconciling both trade and margin statements to internal records? Reconciliation should be done by someone with access to trade data so errors are not overlooked. This person should not be responsible for trades.

- For exchange-traded derivatives, who is responsible for the margin account? Can a margin call be responded to if this person is not available?

- How are transaction limits and authority established for staff? Position limits and authority for transactions should be clearly stipulated. Appropriate authority should also exist in the event that key personnel are unavailable.

- Who is responsible for keeping counterparties (e.g., financial institutions) informed of trading and transaction limits at least annually and on departure of transacting personnel? Notice should be in writing.

- What schedule, if any, should be developed for positions and hedges to be adjusted or refined?

- How and against what benchmark will the performance of hedging strategy be measured?

- What contribution can other departments make to the risk management process? Sales or purchasing departments may have fixed-price contracts with customers or suppliers. They may also be involved with pricing and therefore exchange rates or commodity prices. These individuals often have competitive insight into their markets that may be useful in financial decision making.

- Who is responsible for policies and oversight for market risk management? What limits apply to market risk management? How often will the policy be revisited?

- Who is responsible for policies and oversight for credit risk management? What level of creditworthiness for a financial institution is acceptable? What limits apply to credit risk management? How often will the policy be revisited?

- What is the policy for obtaining prices from financial institutions when doing transactions? Many organizations use two or more financial institutions to obtain competitive price quotes, dividing larger transactions between them and alternating smaller transactions.

- How comfortable is senior management with policy and prospective risk management strategies? Does management have access to financial decision makers for questions or concerns?

- Are there opportunities for reducing risk by pooling activities with other divisions or branches for netting or other risk-reduction activities? Are these activities permitted by law and regulation in jurisdictions where they are being considered?

- Are the organization's current credit facilities adequate for its use of over-the-counter risk management products and strategies?

- Are dealer and financial institution relationships adequate to provide adequate risk management products and services? Are the organization's financial institutions committed to it and its industry or sector? Discussions with financial institutions may uncover concerns or solutions.

Summary

- It is critical to consider an organization's risk profile in the development of a risk management policy, since risk profile will affect its risk tolerance and appropriate strategies.

- An organization's risk profile is derived from its unique attributes, including its stakeholders, competitors and industry, organizational culture, and financial exposures.

- A hedging policy provides a framework and formalized strategies for managing risk to facilitate day-to-day decision making.

- An independent risk oversight function gives management a level of comfort and answers the question, "Who is looking after risk management?"

CHAPTER 9

Measuring Risk

After reading this chapter you will be able to

- Differentiate between measures of exposure and measures of risk
- Consider the strengths and weaknesses of risk measurement methodologies
- Identify alternative strategies for estimating risks

Risk is the business of probabilities, and risk measurement is one component of risk management. Risk management involves identifying and measuring risk, followed by decisions about how best to manage it. Attempts to measure risk involve estimating the probability of an adverse event occurring and its potential impact. Volatility estimates are typically calculated using variance or standard deviation around the mean.

Measures of Exposure

To reduce risk, it is necessary to manage exposure. Measures of risk and exposure are one component of risk management and start with the following central questions:

- What is the exposure?

- How sensitive is the exposure?

- How much can I lose?

Market risk is the risk of an adverse movement in the price or value of a commodity, currency, or asset. Market risk measurement has primarily been developed in the financial institution sector, but methods have increasingly been adopted by other organizations. Quantifying risk is a complex topic, and this chapter will highlight some key points.

There are two views of risk management. The first is from the day-to-day or tactical standpoint. The second is a high-level or strategic view. In order to manage risk, it is necessary to have the capability to monitor risk from both standpoints in order to assess potential loss to the organization.

How Much Can I Lose?

There are several ways to estimate potential loss. The concept of probability is the central tenet of risk, and the business of risk measurement involves estimating the likely variability of returns. The term *risk measurement* is a bit of a misnomer. Risk measurement is an attempt to answer the question, "How much can I lose?" with reasonable certainty.

Quantitative techniques and rigorous processes can overshadow more mundane sources of significant risk and the need for common sense. Although attention must be paid to internal sources of risk, such as operational controls, other risks arise from external events and may be beyond the control of organizations that seek to manage them.

Risk management requires both quantitative and qualitative analysis. Unfortunately, risk management cannot be reduced to a simple checklist, process, or a single number. Trying to do so can create a mechanistic approach to risk management when one of imagination is needed.

Process of Estimating Risk

The estimation of risk is a two-part process. The first part of the process is estimating the likely gain, or—more importantly in risk management—the likely loss, from changes in market rates or prices. To calculate potential loss, it is necessary to estimate the sensitivity of the instrument or exposure to market changes. Measures such as duration (for interest rates) are useful to estimate sensitivity to market changes.

The second part of the process involves estimating the probability of the aforementioned market changes. Given a potential change in market rates and the size of the underlying position, plus the probability of the change in market rates occurring, the potential loss (or gain) can be estimated. Alter any of the constituents of the assessment, and a different potential loss may result.

Gap Analysis

Gap or mismatch analysis measures the sensitivity of an exposure, asset, or portfolio to market rate or price changes by considering the mismatch between assets and liabilities. When there is a mismatch between assets and liabilities, or cash inflows and cash outflows, there is exposure and an opportunity for loss.

Gap analysis is traditionally undertaken by financial institutions managing the balance of assets to liabilities. A financial institution that wants to minimize the gap between its assets (loans and mortgages made to customers) and liabilities (deposits and accounts of customers) will group the financial assets and liabilities into maturity *buckets* or pools based on their frequency of repricing or rate resetting. Maturity pools that have significantly more assets than liabilities (or vice versa) are sources of exposure.

Gap analysis can also be used to determine currency exposure arising from foreign currency cash flows. For example, if an organization has more euro inflows than outflows in a given period, but the mismatch reverses the following period, then the euro cash flows offset one another with only a timing difference. If over the course of a longer period, such as a fiscal cycle, there are more euros coming in than going out, the difference provides exposure to a falling euro.

Leverage and Direction

The use of leverage increases the potential for loss. Therefore, the impact of any leverage or gearing strategy is important to consider when calculating the amount that an organization could potentially lose. The calculation of potential loss without considering the impact of leverage underestimates potential losses.

Direction is the nature of an exposure or trading position, either long or short. A long position will obviously benefit from a rise in prices, while a short position benefits from a price decline. Both leverage and direction are factors in the potential size of a loss given an adverse market move.

Instrument Sensitivity

Measures of instrument sensitivity can be a useful way to measure potential for risk. Duration provides an estimate of the sensitivity of fixed income securities' prices to small changes in interest rates. Duration is also used for assessing gaps between assets and liabilities, since a timing mismatch is a source of interest rate risk. Duration has some limitations, particularly that it works better for small changes in rates. Convexity, which measures the rate of change of duration, can be used to further refine the sensitivity of a fixed income security or exposure to interest rate changes.

Option delta is another measure of sensitivity. The option delta measures the sensitivity of the option's value given a change in the price of the underlying. Options that have little likelihood of exercise because their strike prices are far out-of-the-money have little sensitivity to changes in the price of the underlying asset. These options will therefore have a small delta. Options that have a greater likelihood of exercise will have a higher delta. The delta itself is subject to change, and is measured using gamma, which is the rate of change of delta.

Scenario Analysis

Scenario analysis (what–if analysis) offers a useful way to assess potential loss by analyzing the value of an instrument or portfolio under different, arbitrarily determined scenarios. Correlations are dynamic, not static, and therefore different correlation assumptions are used in different scenarios. In scenario analysis, it is necessary to make some assumptions about correlation, but a range of assumptions should be used in the different scenarios. In a crisis scenario, markets may become highly correlated with one another, increasing potential for loss.

Scenario analysis is straightforward and involves using a set of predetermined changes in market prices or rates (scenarios) to test the performance of the current portfolio or exposure. Most financial managers already perform ad-hoc scenario analysis calculations when determining potential outcomes of various decisions, markets, or transactions.

Scenarios may be one-factor scenarios, for example, assessing the results of a change in interest rates, or they may be multifactor, permitting a range of interest rate scenarios combined with a change in foreign exchange rates and a change in revenues. Specialized software permits several different scenarios to be run simultaneously, with the results providing information about the potential for loss (or gain) under different scenarios, although simple scenarios can be captured in more basic software.

Modern scenario analysis generally assumes some asset correlation into future market movements, which is adequate when the scenarios are those that might be anticipated in a relatively normal market. Indeed, hedging itself is an attempt to protect the business activities of an organization from market risk.

Scenario analysis can be used to determine how assets will perform in relation to one another under relatively normal market conditions. Most traders use scenario analysis to assess strategic and tactical exposure. Scenario analysis is a useful methodology that can be used by all financial managers.

IN THE REAL WORLD

Stress Situations

Scenario analysis is useful under ordinary circumstances involving routine market changes. However, in crisis situations financial markets may behave differently than they would be expected to. In severe market conditions, there is a danger that correlational relationships may break down. For example, markets that are expected to have low correlation may become highly correlated, at least in the short term.

In extreme situations or in markets where liquidity is marginal to begin with, liquidity may dry up completely for a short time. Without knowing how these relationships may change under duress, scenario analysis may not provide a complete picture of the portfolio's risk.

Scenario analysis is a useful adjunct to value-at-risk for risk measurement. Scenario analysis allows a risk manager to determine how a portfolio would behave under a predetermined set of scenarios. For example, using a set of arbitrary market scenarios to test the performance of a bond portfolio, a risk manager may determine the impact of a 50-basis-point parallel shift (up or down) in the yield curve. Scenario analysis is intuitively appealing because it answers the *what-if* part of the risk measurement question.

Although scenario analysis is intuitively appealing, it has limitations. For example, while a scenario of a 50-basis-point increase in interest rates might be useful, in the real world, yield curves do not shift in parallel. In real life, yield curves steepen and flatten in unpredictable ways across the maturity spectrum, and therefore not all models may fully capture such moves. As a result, a portfolio's changes should be evaluated under different yield curve scenarios, such as the following:

- Parallel shift with rising interest rates

- Parallel shift with declining interest rates

- Steepening of the yield curve, assuming a normal yield curve (longer rates rise more than shorter rates)

- Flattening of the yield curve, assuming a normal yield curve (longer rates rise less than shorter rates)

From a management standpoint, scenario analysis may facilitate management discussion and quantification of acceptable risk levels. A formalized discussion of risk is usually beneficial from a risk management perspective.

Stress Testing

Stress testing is similar to scenario analysis but is designed to assess performance under less frequent, but more significant, market moves. Stress testing permits the risk manager to determine how a series of exposures would perform under additional conditions. A stress test may involve changing one or more variables or using major historical price changes to assess the potential impact to a financial instrument or portfolio.

Large moves often take market participants by surprise, and markets may move farther and faster than would otherwise be expected. These large moves may be combined with a breakdown in the typical correlational relationships that are present during normal market conditions.

Stress testing an organization's exposure can be very useful. In the event that the stress test shows unacceptable results in the form of unmanageable potential losses, strategies can be formulated to deal with the exposures and potential risks.

Financial Crises

Although financial crises occur with regularity, they are unfortunately not predictable. As a result, organizations should consider the ramifications of extraordinary market events, to the extent possible, in their risk management planning. This means ensuring an adequate financial risk management framework is in place, understanding current exposures, and avoiding overreliance on probability-based measures of risk.

Financial crises may be localized or global. Their attributes are similar:

- They occur relatively frequently.

- They are not predictable.

- Ordinary relationships, such as correlations between markets and instruments, may break down entirely.

- Proper preparation is required, including a risk management policy and an action plan.

- Systemic risk becomes the major concern to central banks and regulators.

The pressures leading to a crisis may be visible for some time prior to the triggering event. In financial crisis situations, ordinary relationships between markets may break down, exacerbating the effects of the crisis. It may be difficult to obtain market prices or information, and it may be costly to initiate or close out transactions. Liquidity and lines of credit often become quite scarce, and volatilities and spreads widen dramatically.

Some experts believe that financial institution consolidation may increase the risk of financial crisis. As consolidation reduces the number of market participants, it increases the likelihood that portfolios or positions of remaining large participants will be similar. Fewer differentiated participants may result in less portfolio and position diversity and greater risk of a crisis.

Value-at-Risk

The most commonly used measure of market risk is value-at-risk. Value-at-risk is a systematic methodology to quantify potential financial loss based on statistical estimates of probability. An estimate of the

IN THE REAL WORLD

Notable Quote

"The key to truly effective risk management lies in the behavior of markets during times of crisis, when investment value is most at risk. Observing markets under stress teaches important lessons about the role and dynamics of markets and the implications for risk management."

Source: Richard M. Bookstaber, "A Framework for Understanding Market Crisis," *Risk Management, Principles, and Practices*, AIMR Conference Proceeding, no. 3, 1999. Copyright 1999, CFA Institute.

probability of a loss being greater than (or less than) a particular dollar amount as a result of market fluctuations, value-at-risk is commonly used to measure risk in a portfolio of assets or exposures.

Value-at-risk attempts to answer the question, "How much money might I lose?" based on probabilities and within parameters set by the risk manager. Value-at-risk calculations are based on one of several methods.

Value-at-risk creates a distribution of potential outcomes at a specified confidence interval. The largest loss outcome using the confidence level as the cut-off is the amount reported as value-at risk. Confidence intervals are typically 95, 97.5, or 99 percent. For example, at a 95 percent confidence interval, there is the probability of a loss being greater than $10,000,000 on 5 days out of 100 days.

Though the idea of a single number to quantify risk is inherently attractive, there are limitations in its use. Most important, it is possible to lose more than the value-at-risk amount. Value-at-risk is only one risk measurement tool, and it should be used in conjunction with a range of other risk measurement tools. Scenario analysis is one useful adjunct to value-at-risk.

IN THE REAL WORLD

Notable Quote

"No amount of observations of white swans can allow the inference that all swans are white, but the observation of a single black swan is sufficient to refute that conclusion."

Source: Dave Hume, "Treatise on Human Nature." Quoted by Nassim Nicholas Taleb, *Fooled By Randomness—The Hidden Role of Chance in the Markets and in Life* (New York: Texere LLC, 2001), p. 100. Copyright 2001 by Nassim Nicholas Taleb.

TIPS & TECHNIQUES

Risk Measurement
Model Challenges

There are risks involved with the reliance on risk measurement models. Issues to consider include:

- Data accuracy and availability issues

- Extreme price events that are infrequent but need analysis

- Ability to reflect optionality, including embedded options

- Overreliance on quantitative without understanding qualitative risk issues

Value-at-risk provides an estimate of the riskiness of a portfolio. In estimating potential for losses, value-at-risk provides information about portfolio weaknesses and exposures that can be subsequently addressed by the risk management group.

Although value-at-risk is a useful measure because of its ability to distill a great deal of information into a single number, there are strengths and weaknesses associated with it. Clearly, one of the key advantages of value-at-risk is its ability to focus both nonfinancial and financial managers on the issue of measuring risk. Despite its shortcomings, it may encourage a more systematic and multidimensional approach to financial risk.

Methods to Calculate Value-at-Risk

There are several ways to calculate value-at-risk. The methods vary in their need for market data, the computing power required, and the ability

IN THE REAL WORLD

A Short History of Value–at–Risk

The widespread use of value-at-risk for risk management purposes is relatively new. The Group of 30's seminal 1993 *Practices and Principles* report recommended measuring market risk using value-at-risk with a standard time horizon and confidence interval (recommendations are found in Chapter 7). A survey that same year found only 5 percent of firms disclosed value-at-risk estimates to shareholders. Four short years later, the proportion had increased to 81 percent. The market was onto something.

Financial institutions had been working with value-at-risk variations for some time. However, J.P. Morgan's development of RiskMetrics[a] methodology for calculating value-at-risk was a major milestone in the evolution of risk measurement. Its introduction in 1994 provided many firms with their first exposure to value-at-risk. Originally known as the "4:15 report" because of the time it was delivered each afternoon, RiskMetrics was developed to give J.P. Morgan's new chief executive officer, Sir Dennis Weatherstone, a clear measure and view of the risks being taken by the firm's various activities.

The methodology, which had been developed internally for the firm's own market risk measurement, enabled virtually any firm to test-drive value-at-risk using the parametric approach. In doing so, it promoted a new approach to market risk transparency and provided a risk measurement benchmark. As a result, it was beneficial to both clients and the broader market. Value-at-risk has gained tremendous support from the to model different types of instruments. Value-at-risk calculations are typically obtained using one of the following methods:

- Using historical data

- Using stochastic simulation, random or Monte Carlo scenario generation. Monte Carlo simulation is based on randomly generated market moves. Volatilities and correlations are calculated directly from underlying time-series data, assuming a normal distribution.

- Value-at-risk using the variance/covariance (parametric) approach. Volatilities and correlations are calculated directly from the underlying time series, assuming a normal distribution.

Assumptions and Limitations

Value-at-risk calculations introduce some important assumptions and limitations. These assumptions and limitations should be understood in the context of their implications for measuring and managing risk.

Financial markets, and in particular, the returns of many assets, are not normally distributed. Rather, there is a tendency to have larger outlying results (known as *fat tails*) than would be expected with a normal distribution, and peaks around the mean. Large losses are more likely, and typically more important to the risk manager, than gains of the same magnitude.

In addition, most value-at-risk models make the assumption that returns each period—each day, for example—are independent of one another, which market history shows is not always the case. The market's behavior yesterday has much more impact on today's prices than events last year.

Depending on the methodology used, the calculation of value-at-risk can be quite demanding. For example, the computing power required to analyze a portfolio of cash flows for thousands of instruments for a large financial institution or trading house is not insignificant.

Although a single risk number is intuitively attractive, its simplicity is also a limitation. Value-at-risk does not consider all risk factors, nor does it perform well as a risk measure for nontraded exposures. It also does not consider how market correlations might change or disintegrate under extreme conditions in a financial crisis. As a result, risk measures are at best an estimate of potential loss.

TIPS & TECHNIQUES

Senior Management

Senior management and the board of directors must be cognizant of value-at-risk's meaning when presented regularly with reports that appear to quantify maximum loss based on risk measures such as value-at-risk. There may be a weak understanding of the concept of value-at-risk. In particular, it may be poorly understood that there is a small probability of losses much greater than models predict. In addition, management may not fully comprehend the importance of non-market risks, such as operational failures, that can also result in significant losses.

Risk measurement may convey a false sense of security among management that financial risks have been measured and that they are therefore being managed appropriately. Risk measurement is only one component of risk management, and many organizations have been good at measuring risk but poor at managing it. Markets are always capable of unexpected results. As a result, best efforts at measuring risk will never fully capture potential future outcomes, even if estimates are good most of the time. The occasional poor estimate of risk may be the proverbial iceberg.

Value-at-Risk Using Historical Simulation

One way to calculate value-at-risk is to use past returns to simulate future returns as a guide to estimating potential loss. Under historical simulation value-at-risk, the portfolio is repriced for a predetermined number of historical periods (e.g., 200 days).

The resultant returns, ranked by magnitude from best to worst, provide a snapshot of the portfolio's value under historical market data with the worst results commonly at the 95 percent level (excluding the worst 5 percent of returns) or the 99 percent level (excluding the worst 1 percent of returns). The worst returns are the ones that most interest the risk manager. The result provides useful information about the risks associated with the current portfolio based on historical market movements.

There are advantages to the simplicity of historical simulation for the calculation of value-at-risk. The methodology is relatively intuitive and easy to understand. It does not make assumptions about the future shape of distributions of returns, volatility, or the correlations of returns between assets other than those that are implied by past returns. As a result, the historical simulation method is suitable for portfolios with nonlinear instruments, such as options.

However, historical data available may not be representative of the market over the long term, and markets can change over time. In addition, the historical data may not contain an appropriate market event, or it may be subject to an ongoing directional price trend. The historical period may not have exhibited any unusually large movements or the kinds of moves that a financial manager might wish to observe in the portfolio.

Value-at-Risk Using Monte Carlo Simulation

Monte Carlo simulation involves computing value-at-risk using tools that automatically generate large numbers of random price or rate changes. These price changes are applied to the portfolio of assets or exposures and the results are measured. The worst results of the resulting distribution are considered the value-at-risk amount, using a specified confidence level.

One advantage of Monte Carlo simulation is that it allows a financial manager to use the results of hundreds or thousands of scenarios to calculate value-at-risk. The resultant frequency distribution can be used to determine value-at-risk with the desired confidence interval.

The risk manager can specify distributions and parameters, or use historical or forecast volatility data, depending on the requirements. Although it is an extremely useful tool, the analysis of large or complex portfolios requires adequate technology to be effective, as computational complexity may be high depending on the portfolio's constituents.

To better understand computational requirements, consider a portfolio of long-term interest rate swaps. Swap values depend on the present value of the cash flows associated with them. Each swap may have dozens of future cash flows. Repricing thousands of swaps in a value-at-risk simulation with a thousand or more scenarios is not an insignificant task.

Monte Carlo simulations are typically accomplished using specialized software. Innovations in technology and simulation have made the calculations using Monte Carlo simulation for large, complex portfolios more accessible and cost effective.

Value-at-Risk Using the Parametric Approach

The parametric approach to calculating value-at-risk is also known as the variance/covariance method, the correlation method, or the analytical method. Of the parametric models available, the best known is probably RiskMetrics.

The parametric approach to value-at-risk has origins in modern portfolio theory, where the risk of a portfolio of assets is assumed to be a function of the risk or variability of each instrument in the portfolio and the correlations between instruments in the portfolio.

The parametric value-at-risk methodology is often combined with another methodology for analyzing the behavior of nonlinear instruments and exposures. The traditional parametric approach is not effective for all types of assets or instruments such as options.

Credit Risk Measurement

Credit risk is the probability of loss as a result of the failure or unwillingness of a counterparty or borrower to fulfill a financial obligation. Exposure to credit risk increases with the market value of outstanding financial instruments with other counterparties, all else being equal.

Counterparty Ratings

Financial institutions have significant exposure to credit risk due to the nature of their various activities and the number of transactions involved. Due to their exposure, these financial institutions tend to be at the forefront of credit risk measurement and management.

The traditional management of credit risk entailed monitoring many aspects of a borrower's affairs. One of the most fundamental aspects of credit risk management today is the careful selection of an appropriate counterparty. In trading, the selection of counterparties is very important. Counterparties with financial stability, acceptable ratings, familiarity, political stability, satisfactory geographical location, and appropriate legal form of organization are chosen.

The global financial community extensively uses ratings provided by major rating agencies. These companies rate specific securities offerings, typically debt, and are used by institutional investors such as mutual and hedge fund managers, lenders, and individual investors. Ratings are used to assess creditworthiness and thus the likelihood of a default by the issuer. They are not a substitute for counterparty risk management.

Organizations monitoring credit risk may require that trading counterparties, issuers, or potential creditors have a minimum acceptable rating from at least one of the major ratings agencies.

Notional Exposure

Notional, contractual, or nominal amounts outstanding are sometimes cited as amounts at risk. Depending on the source of the exposure, however, such an assessment may be too simplistic. In traditional creditor roles, such as lending, trade receivables, or similar, the full notional amount is at risk because the borrower or debtor may choose not to pay amounts owed. The notional amount of the debt then becomes the potential loss, less any residual collections that can be made.

With many derivatives transactions, such as interest rate swap where net payments are made between counterparties, less than the notional amount may be at risk. For other derivatives, such as currency swaps, payments may be more significant, and the full amount may be at risk, especially during settlement.

Notional amounts are important in the discussion of settlement risk. When both counterparties to a trade settle in full by making pay-

IN THE REAL WORLD

NRSRO Rating Agencies

There are credit rating agencies in major countries around the world. Agencies whose credit ratings are used under the U.S. Securities and Exchange Commission (SEC) regulations are known as nationally recognized statistical rating organizations (NRSROs):

- Dominion Bond Rating Service Limited (DBRS), www.dbrs.com

- Fitch, Inc., www.fitchratings.com

- Moody's Investors Service, Inc., www.moodys.com

- Standard & Poor's Ratings Services (S&P), www.standardandpoors.com

Debt offerings of many governments and corporations are rated by one or more of these rating agencies, which may change from time to time. Issuers pay to be rated by agencies. Although the use of ratings published by independent rating agencies provides some guidance, it is not infallible, and there have been unexpected and spectacular failures of rated organizations. More information can be obtained from the SEC.

ments to one another, the failure of one counterparty to pay could result in the loss of the entire notional amount to the other counterparty. Settlement risk gives rise to the potential for a loss of the notional amount, and therefore it should be managed carefully.

Aggregate Exposure

Given the importance of credit risk in both derivatives and nonderivatives transactions, it is important to be able to determine total exposure to a counterparty at any point in time and compare these aggregates to established in-house counterparty limits. This is a key measure to monitor an organization's exposure.

Organizations should aggregate credit exposure to individual counterparties. Aggregate totals can be netted in those situations where there is a legally enforceable netting agreement in place between the counterparties and for the transactions.

Replacement Cost

Both current and potential exposures that arise from derivatives contracts can be assessed. Current exposure, or replacement cost, can be determined by reviewing the market value of outstanding contracts. The marked-to-market or current value can be considered a measure of replacement cost and therefore a measure of risk. If the derivatives counterparty defaulted on its obligations, replacement cost measures the cost to replicate the position at current market prices, presuming no settlement issues. Potential exposure can be calculated using probability analysis.

Credit Risk Measures

Credit risk measures are based on probability estimates of loss resulting from a default. They depend on the probability of the counterparty defaulting, the organization's exposure to the defaulting counterparty at the time of default, and any amounts that can be recovered after default. These individual determinants of credit risk can be summarized as:

- Probability of counterparty default, which is an assessment of the likelihood of the counterparty defaulting

- Exposure at counterparty default, which takes into account an organization's exposure to a defaulting counterparty at the time of default

- Loss given counterparty default, which considers recovery of amounts that reduces the loss otherwise resulting from a default

Default risk, or the probability that a default occurs or does not occur, is modeled by many organizations, including rating agencies. Although a default can be modeled as an independent event, losses from defaults often depend on both the probability of an individual default and the correlation between defaults of different counterparties or obligations.

Credit value-at-risk provides a distribution of potential credit losses over a specified time horizon and examines the credit value-at-risk at a particular confidence interval. The risk manager can then review those exposures that contribute significantly to an organization's credit risk and take remedial action, if necessary.

Credit derivatives markets reflect the assessment of risk by market participants. Prices based on actual transactions between relatively sophisticated participants may provide insight into the market's assessment of the riskiness of an organization. Therefore, prices such as those of credit default swaps may be a useful adjunct to other credit risk measures.

Future of Credit Risk Measurement

Major steps are being taken in the development of various quantitative methodologies to model and measure credit risk. In part, the revised Basel II framework for capital requirements has led to the implementation of highly sophisticated credit risk management capabilities on a global scale and the improvement of existing methodologies. These credit risk measurement and management capabilities will inevitably filter down from large financial institutions to smaller organizations. Basel II is discussed in more detail in Chapter 10.

Operational Risk Measurement

Operational risk, which is discussed in more detail in Chapter 7, results from an organization's exposure to people, processes, and systems. Operational risk management exists to reduce the possibility of fraud or error resulting in loss to the organization. Many of the large bank trading losses that have been widely reported in the media have been due to operational failures.

Some methods that have been used to measure or indicate potential for operational risk in financial institutions and other organizations include:

- Number of deviations from policy or stated procedures

- Comments and notes from internal or external audits

- Volume of derivatives trades (gross, not netted)

- Levels of staff turnover

- Volatility of earnings

- Unusual complaints from customers or vendors

Increasingly, operational risk databases are used to model operational risk for probability of occurrence and aid in risk reduction. The operational risk database is used to identify and assess potential risks and track their occurrence. Resulting data can be used as an input to model operational risk occurrence probabilities and potential losses. For operational risk events, the probability of an individual occurrence may be small but have potential for a significant loss.

In related audit and fraud prevention areas, probability assessments are also used. In addition, the insurance industry quantifies particular operational risks in order to price various types of insurance coverage. However, this expertise is relatively specialized and usually beyond the scope of general financial risk management.

Summary

- The concept of probability is the central tenet of risk, and the business of risk measurement involves estimating the probability of loss.

- Scenario analysis involves using a set of predetermined changes in market prices or scenarios to test the performance of the current portfolio or exposure.

- The most commonly used measure of market risk is value-at-risk, a systematic methodology based on statistical estimates.

- As the costs of computation decline and user sophistication increases, the number and variety of risk management tools has increased substantially. More rigorous measurements of risk will likely become commonplace.

CHAPTER 10

Global Initiatives in Financial Risk Management

After reading this chapter you will be able to

- Understand the challenges that exist in financial risk management
- Identify initiatives for reducing risk in key areas such as settlements, trading, and payments
- Appreciate the significance of accounting and regulatory initiatives
- Evaluate how changes in capital adequacy can reduce systemic risk

In a global marketplace, there are many opportunities for risk. Losses may not be limited to one geographical or domestic market but could potentially arise due to a failure in settlement, regional financial crisis, or an unexpected geopolitical event almost anywhere. Efforts being made today are intended to ensure that global financial markets can cope with increased interconnectedness and the resultant risks in many types of market conditions.

Challenges

Financial institutions, due to the nature of their business activities and volume of transactions, have natural exposure to many financial risks. As a result, many risk management initiatives—such as credit risk, settlement, and payment system initiatives—have been introduced by or for financial institutions.

Financial risk management is made all the more challenging by the fact that many organizations face global markets of significant size, complexity of participants and transactions, different legal and regulatory systems, and myriad unknown factors.

Several major international initiatives have been undertaken to reduce financial risk and therefore systemic risk. International initiatives by regulators, payments associations, central banks, and financial institutions to reduce opportunities for risk include:

- Financial institution capital based on risk

- More secure settlement between counterparties

- Trading initiatives to reflect risk-reduction techniques

- Changes in the operation of international payment systems

International central banks and regulators have been motivated to develop new standards and requirements because of the potential losses associated with financial risk on a large, interconnected global scale. More than volumes, it is the interconnectedness and prevalence of linkages that makes many risk managers uneasy. The challenge is systemic risk.

Financial Institutions

Financial institutions participate in a variety of financial market activities besides lending. Some significant activities include trading in currencies, interest rates, equity and fixed income securities, and a variety of derivatives, both on a proprietary interbank basis and on behalf of their customers.

In addition to market risk, trading exposes a financial institution to significant operational and credit risk. A financial institution may have hundreds or thousands of trades per day. As a result, there is exposure to the possibility of default or failure of other financial institutions, as well as of nonfinancial institutions. These exposures have given rise to the need for new techniques for managing risk, and, in particular, credit risk.

Derivatives Trading

Derivatives trading volumes show no signs of slowing down. Even with occasional slowing growth in a region or market, rapid growth in many markets is ongoing. From a segmented market perspective, foreign exchange volumes remain the largest in the world. However, in over-the-counter derivatives, interest rate derivatives, particularly swaps, are the most popular.

IN THE REAL WORLD

Over-the-Counter Derivatives

In the over-the-counter derivatives market where much of the trading between financial institutions, corporations, and investment funds occurs, volumes are much larger than in the listed market.

According to the International Swaps and Derivatives Association (ISDA), an international organization of more than 600 financial institutions that tracks such statistics, outstanding over-the-counter interest rate derivatives were about U.S.$164 trillion in mid-2004.

Other outstanding derivatives include credit derivatives at $5 trillion and equity derivatives at nearly $4 trillion (both amounts in U.S. dollars).

Statistics such as trading volume and amounts outstanding do not necessarily represent amounts at risk. In many cases, the amounts at risk during settlement or as a result of default may be significantly smaller than the amounts traded.

Many contracts call for netted payments between counterparties or differential payments. For example, in an interest rate swap, the notional amount of the contract is not exchanged between the counterparties, significantly reducing settlement risk. In such cases, settlement risk is much less of an issue, although other risks such as market risk and replacement risk remain a concern.

Credit Risk

Credit exposure exists within most organizations, but it is especially significant in major financial institutions. As a result, financial institutions and their regulators are the source of many credit risk management initiatives, in particular Basel II, which is leading to the implementation of highly sophisticated credit risk management capabilities on a global scale.

Financial institutions and their customers are connected through their business activities with one another to a greater magnitude today than in the past. Credit risk is closely tied to systemic risk, where the failure of one or more major counterparties could trigger other failures.

One of the most fundamental aspects of credit risk management is the careful selection of a counterparty. In trading, the selection of counterparties is very important. Successful financial institutions screen and select counterparties and borrowers based on financial stability, ratings, familiarity, political stability, geographical location, and legal form of organization.

Enterprisewide Risk Management

The concept of enterprisewide risk management has been around for more than a decade. It involves organizations taking a broad and

IN THE REAL WORLD

Counterparty Risk Management Policy Group

The 1999 report published by the Counterparty Risk Management Policy Group in conjunction with the International Swaps and Derivatives Association (ISDA) addressed ways to improve counterparty risk management practices. Developed with a dozen major international banks, it is intended to promote enhanced counterparty credit and market risk practices among organizations involved in derivatives trading.

The report is aimed at financial institutions, investment managers, insurance companies, and hedge funds and includes specific recommendations for managing counterparty credit risk. These recommendations include measures to improve transparency and counterparty credit assessment, improve risk measurement and management, enhance risk reporting, and provide better market practices and conventions. In addition, the document outlines recommendations for improving regulatory reporting. The document can be viewed on the ISDA Web site at www.isda.org.

strategic view of all risks, including financial risks, business risks, and other related risks.

The goal of enterprisewide risk management is certainly a worthy one. The ability to measure an organization's exposure to a wide variety of risks, report on them, and use the information to make decisions throughout an organization is an excellent objective.

One of the challenges with enterprisewide risk management is the need to measure and estimate probabilities of loss for which a strong risk management framework does not exist. Risks associated with insurance have been monitored and measured for decades by the industry. Financial risks have an advantage in that many years of study and analysis have been expended in order to better estimate them. Given that the estimation of risk is good only at the best of times, other risks may require similar time and experience to determine appropriate measures.

Settlement Initiatives

Continuous Linked Settlement

Trading in financial instruments and derivatives gives rise to settlement risk because each counterparty to a transaction faces the possibility of not being paid during settlement. Traditionally, large global trading volumes resulted in large settlements between trading counterparties, primarily large financial institutions.

Trading and settlement occurs between counterparties in international financial centers and different time zones. Settlements are made electronically, involving national payments systems and local banks for final crediting or debiting of accounts.

Potential losses arising from failure to settle are exacerbated when counterparties are located in different time zones and from settling currency transactions. Currency settlements often involve currencies in different global regions, such as Asia and North America, for example. This means that most settlement occurs nonsimultaneously during the 24-hour day, since it depends on local processing in the financial center where payments are initiated.

A major initiative to reduce the settlement risk associated with payments arising from foreign exchange settlements is continuous linked settlement (CLS), which began operations in 2002 and is supported by several dozen of the world's largest banks.

Foreign Exchange Trading

Foreign exchange trading volumes eclipse other types of trading. The 2004 triennial survey by central banks and the Bank for International Settlements (BIS) shows daily volumes of about U.S.$1.9 trillion. A significant proportion of this foreign exchange volume is interbank trading.

CLS Bank International is a special-purpose bank, central to the system and based in New York. The system operates a multicurrency settlement facility into which payments between financial institutions are made. CLS Bank connects to the real-time gross settlement systems operated by the central banks in each currency's home country. Within CLS Bank is an account for each currency.

With CLS, since trading and settlement occur in different time zones, it is necessary to find a short window of the 24-hour day when all regions can connect simultaneously. CLS uses a five-hour overlap time and links to country's local real-time gross settlement systems to settle for a particular date as though both parties were in the same time zone. CLS Bank works simultaneously with the various national payment systems during the time window when all the participating national payment systems are operational.

The *pay-in period* sees CLS member banks make payments to CLS Bank in currencies they owe to other counterparties. At the start of the payment period, each member bank receives a schedule detailing the net positions in each currency. Payments are made on a net basis. Simultaneous settlement, also known as a payment-versus-payment basis, is accomplished as funds are credited to CLS member banks that are expecting payment.

IN THE REAL WORLD

Continuous
Linked Settlement

Continuous linked settlement is supported by several dozen of the world's leading financial institutions. It permits simultaneous settlement of foreign exchange transactions between counterparties, significantly reducing risk. Although additional currencies are planned for implementation, 15 currencies are currently eligible for CLS settlement as of 2005:

1. Australian dollar	**9.** New Zealand dollar
2. British pound	**10.** Norwegian krone
3. Canadian dollar	**11.** South African rand
4. Danish krone	**12.** Singapore dollar
5. Euro	**13.** Swedish krona
6. Hong Kong dollar	**14.** Swiss franc
7. Japanese yen	**15.** U.S. dollar
8. Korean won	

The system provides a simultaneous settlement to both parties, providing assurance that parties to a transaction will receive value for their payment. Like the payments made by the national payment systems, CLS payments are made with finality and are irrevocable.

By the end of 2004, CLS had settled more than $3.6 trillion on a single record day, with $1.9 trillion representative of an average day. This represents a significant proportion of daily foreign exchange and derivatives settlement volume. With this volume comes a reduction in nonsimultaneous settlement risk, and an increase in control over liquidity because banks can see exactly when settlements will occur.

Users of CLS include major banks and investment custodial firms operating on behalf of fund managers. Nonfinancial institutions typically participate through a financial institution.

Trading Initiatives

Derivatives are contractual agreements, and the integrity of each counterparty and the likelihood of it performing its obligations under predetermined terms of the contract are paramount.

Users of exchange-traded derivatives have relied for many years on specific risk management processes. Exchanges employ various mechanisms to manage risk, among them clearinghouses for settling exchange trades. The clearinghouse acts as the guarantor to every trade, including a defaulted trade, as a mechanism to ensure that counterparties fulfill their obligations.

Exchanges also use daily market value of all outstanding positions, margin, and, in most cases, daily maximum price fluctuations. The combination of market value, margin, and price limits provides a theoretical worst-case one-day scenario for the exchange and its clearinghouse.

As derivatives trading volumes have increased, specific efforts have been made to reduce the risks inherent in the trading and settlement of derivatives. The model from exchange-traded derivatives minimizes counterparty risk through straightforward but effective methods.

In the over-the-counter derivatives markets, netting agreements and initiatives such as CLS are similar attempts to reduce counterparty risk. In addition, margin-like collateral and repricing of agreements is taking place more often.

Collateral Usage

Among financial institutions and dealers trading in derivatives, there is an increased use of collateral. Collateral, most commonly cash or government securities, reduces the exposure associated with the potential for default by a counterparty. The use of collateral also permits financial institutions to free up trading credit facilities that might otherwise be unavailable.

A 2004 ISDA survey[i] of collateral use in privately negotiated derivatives transactions and related margined activities found a significant increase in collateral usage. The survey also found that 50 percent of all derivatives transactions, measured either by volume or by exposure, were covered by collateral at the survey date.

The majority of organizations that were surveyed by ISDA are banks. When surveyed about their reasons for the use of collateral in agreements, the most common answer was a reduction of economic capital or credit risk.

New Products

Trading in new products reflects the new realities of business and financial markets. For example, the venerable London Metals Exchange has developed trading products in polypropylene and linear low-density polyethylene plastics. These contracts provide a new way for manufacturers and consumers to manage the financial risk associated with price fluctuations. Like metals contracts, these reflect the economic realities of industry today.

In other markets, inflation derivatives, such as inflation futures and swaps, provide a means for hedging and trading inflation risk separately from market risk and credit risk. The Chicago Mercantile Exchange lists futures contracts on the U.S. Consumer Price Index (CPI) and products also trade in the over-the-counter market.

Weather derivatives usage has increased significantly, both in the over-the-counter and the exchange-traded market. Cooling degree days (CDD) and heating degree days (HDD) allow hedgers and traders to manage temperatures, in addition to regional contracts that cover

TIPS & TECHNIQUES

Weather in Chicago

The Chicago Mercantile Exchange offers a number of weather-related products for hedgers. Futures contracts, and options on futures, are available in three global regions. Among the weather-hedging products are the following:

- CME Seasonal Cooling Degree Days Index

- CME Seasonal Heating Degree Days Index

- European Monthly CAT Index

- European Monthly Heating Degree Day

- European Seasonal CAT Index

- European Seasonal Heating Degree Day

- Japanese Monthly Average Temperature

- Japanese Seasonal Average Temperature

averages or indices. In the over-the-counter market, customized products can be structured to meet the particular need of a hedger.

Other new trading products include environmental derivatives. Environmental derivatives are the current new frontier, and significant growth is likely to occur in this area in the future. Carbon and sulfur emission allowances are now trading at the Chicago Climate Exchange. More growth is likely in this area.

Payment Initiatives

On any given day, millions of payments make their way through various international payments systems. Improvements to payment systems have been made with the intention that the default of even a major financial institution would not adversely affect the rest of the system.

As a result of the exposure that exists within the business of global financial institutions, international initiatives are being undertaken to reduce the possibility of such an occurrence. The players include regulators, payments associations, financial institutions, and central banks. Changes in the way payments occur is one such initiative.

International payments systems are adapting to better manage the risks that arise from an interconnected global financial community. Many electronic systems for large-value payments have migrated to a real-time (or quasi-real-time) environment. This intentional shift may reduce the systemic risk arising from credit and settlement risk in financial transactions, as the risk of a default occurring between bilateral settlements is reduced.

Payment systems in major countries reduce risk through the finality component of the payment. One of the risks associated with older payment systems was that receipt of funds was sometimes uncertain. Payments received could subsequently be reversed at a later date, thus providing little comfort to financial institutions, or their clients, concerned about payment default. As a result, new high-value payment systems offer finality of payment.

Capital Adequacy Initiatives

The impact of fewer, consolidated financial institutions has changed the financial landscape in many countries significantly. One of the particular concerns with respect to consolidation is that risk among financial institutions is now more concentrated, making systemic risk a greater potential issue.

The Basel Accord is an agreement between the central banks of major countries to develop consistent minimum capital standards for financial institutions in those countries. The introduction of capital

Payments Systems

In the United States, two systems facilitate high-value payments. The FedWire system, operated by the U.S. Federal Reserve, processes electronic large-value items with same-day value and finality of settlement.

The Clearing House Interbank Payments System (CHIPS) is operated by The Clearing House in New York, which is owned by a group of international banks. It processes more than U.S.$1.3 trillion in about 260,000 transactions on an average day, the majority resulting from settlement of foreign exchange and Eurodollar trades. The CHIPS system is unique in high-value systems because it can transmit large amounts of remittance information along with payments.

In Canada, high-value payments use the Large Value Transfer System (LVTS), operated by the Canadian Payments Association. The LVTS system provides payments that are final and irrevocable.

The Trans-European Automated Real-time Gross settlement Express Transfer (TARGET) system for high-value euro payments is an interlinking system that connects the domestic real-time gross settlement systems of 16 European countries. These payment systems include those of the 12 euro countries, plus Denmark, Sweden, and the United Kingdom. TARGET is operated by the individual country central banks and the European Central Bank.

adequacy requirements beginning more than a decade ago was a major milestone in financial risk management. "Managing risk at the source," as some called it, represented an international convergence of capital measurement and standards.

Capital requirements are the mandated minimum capital that a financial institution must maintain in relationship to its banking activities. One of the core principles of capital adequacy is that more risky activities should have more capital allocated to them.

Capital adequacy requirements were foremost intended to strengthen the stability of the international financial system, particularly against credit risk (a major risk faced by every financial institution), but also against market risk and operational risk.

Although the Basel Accord is largely unseen, its impact has been felt by financial institutions worldwide. Within the banking system, compliance has meant significant explicit and opportunity costs, with addi-

IN THE REAL WORLD

Notable Quote

"An excessively prescriptive approach is an invitation for regulatory arbitrage and for practices that respect the letter of the standards but violate their spirit. Hence, the major efforts by regulators to develop standards in close cooperation and consultation with the regulated communities in the private sector, to stress the adequacy of risk management processes and to strengthen disclosures. These are all welcome trends that should be encouraged further."

Source: Malcolm Knight, General Manager of the BIS, "Markets and Institutions: Managing the Evolving Risk," speech at the 25th SUERF Colloquium in Madrid, October 14, 2004.

tional costs for amendments to the accord. The increased cost of capital is initially borne by the financial institution, its customers, and its stakeholders, but all market participants benefit from a more secure financial system and ultimately pay for its costs.

Headquartered in Basel, Switzerland, the Bank for International Settlements (BIS) is a central bankers' bank. The Basel Accord is facilitated by the BIS and the Basel Committee on Banking Supervision. The committee consists of senior representatives from banking authorities and central banks from Belgium, Canada, France, Germany, Italy, Japan, Luxembourg, the Netherlands, Spain, Sweden, Switzerland, United Kingdom, and the United States.

Revised Framework

Amendments to the Basel Accord present opportunities to revise the existing system. An amended accord, known as Basel II, was approved in 2004 and involves more risk-sensitive capital requirements.

The new accord permits the additional use of risk assessments by a bank's own internal systems for capital calculations. The accord will not specify risk management policies or practices. Rather, Basel II provides options for banks and banking supervisors to calculate capital requirements for credit risk and operational risk.

Basel II is designed to further increase international banking stability by improving capital adequacy requirements. The new document will require substantially increased sensitivity of the capital requirements to risk. Basel II aligns capital requirements with risk management practices and includes three key areas (called *pillars*):

1. Minimum capital requirements (pillar 1)

2. Supervisory review and processes (pillar 2)

3. Market discipline (pillar 3)

Financial institutions will determine the risk sensitivity of the various transactions on their books, including an assessment of the type of counterparty or borrower. Capital requirements will be based on application of a set of predetermined formulas to the risk data provided by the financial institutions. This includes metrics such as the probability of default (PD), the amount of loss given a default (LGD), the exposure at default (EAD), and maturity assumptions of the various exposures.

Banks can use three approaches for calculating credit risk capital:

1. Standardized approach (regulator provides risk measurement data for probability of default, loss given default, and exposure at default)

2. Foundation Internal Ratings-Based approach (bank provides its own estimate of probability of default, while regulator provides loss given default and exposure at default data)

3. Advanced Internal Ratings-Based approach (bank provides its own probability of default, loss given default, and exposure at default)

Minimum levels of capital will continue to be mandated under Basel II. This means the total amount of regulatory capital will not change but some banks may require less capital and others more, depending on the risk profile of their portfolio. One key issue is that banks will be required to set aside regulatory capital for operational risk under Basel II.

Although minimum capital requirements for financial institutions will not change under Basel II, risk measurement will change. Important changes in the treatment of credit risk will include the recognition that collateral, guarantees, and credit derivatives can be used for credit risk mitigation. In addition, given the importance of retail lending activities for many financial institutions, the accord makes some changes to the risk weightings associated with retail lending, including the risk weighting on mortgages.

IN THE REAL WORLD

Risk Weightings

Basel II necessitates that capital be based on the underlying risk associated with an activity. Consider the following example of risk weightings for claims on sovereigns and central banks in the following table under the standardized approach. These risk weightings use ratings published by Standard & Poor's for illustrative purposes:[a]

Credit Assessment	AAA to AA–	A+ to A–	BBB+ to BBB–	BB+ to B–	Below B–	Unrated
Risk Weight	0%	20%	50%	100%	150%	100%

Basel II is expected to be appropriate for countries and financial institutions beyond the G10 and expected to take effect at the end of 2007. More information on the New Basel Capital Accord, including the original Basel Accord and current documentation, can be found on the BIS web site (www.bis.org).

a "Part 2, First Pillar, Minimum Capital Requirements, II Credit Risk— The Standardized Approach, A (Regulatory Capital), #53," *Basel II: International Convergence of Capital Measurement* and *Capital Standards: A Revised Framework*. Standard & Poor's is a registered trademark of its owners.

Accounting and Regulatory Initiatives

International accounting standards for derivatives continue to evolve toward marking to market and fair value. Regulatory initiatives are attempting to reduce fraudulent activities and reporting, particularly those introduced with the Sarbanes-Oxley Act in the United States and the additional requirements of other countries following Sarbanes-Oxley.

Many organizations have incurred costs in the shift in the accounting treatment of derivatives. However, the changes have also meant a significant increase in transparency for investors and lenders.

FASB 138

In the United States, the Financial Accounting Standards Board (FASB) introduced Statement No. 133, Accounting for Derivative Instruments and Hedging Activities (FASB 133) in 1998, since updated by FASB Statement No. 138. Currently, under U.S. generally accepted accounting principles (GAAP), recognition of gains and losses can be delayed if specific hedge requirements are met, as modifications were made to make it easier to conform for hedging purposes.

IAS 39

The International Accounting Standards Committee Foundation is an oversight body for the International Accounting Standards Board (IASB). IAS Standard 39, which deals with financial instruments, is also a fair value model.

Sarbanes-Oxley Act 2002

The Public Company Accounting and Investor Protection Act of 2002,[ii] also known as Sarbanes-Oxley, has resulted in perhaps the most sweeping reforms in the U.S. securities arena in decades, leading to significant changes in the way that U.S. publicly traded companies undertake business.

The changes and obligations required by Sarbanes-Oxley have resulted in significant implicit and explicit costs for corporations to comply. This is particularly so since the changes went into effect relatively quickly. Since 2002, a number of similar initiatives, though often smaller in scale and less widespread, have been proposed or implemented in other (non-U.S.) jurisdictions.

The Sarbanes-Oxley regulations cover a number of key areas, including the creation of the Public Company Accounting Oversight Board, auditor independence, corporate responsibility, enhanced financial disclosures, analyst conflicts of interest, corporate and criminal fraud accountability, white-collar crime penalty, corporate tax returns, and corporate fraud and accountability.

One area that may be of interest to corporations is the section that deals with enhanced financial disclosures (Title IV of the original document), with the following sections:

401 Disclosures in periodic reports

402 Enhanced conflict-of-interest provisions

403 Disclosures of transactions involving management and principal stockholders

404 Management assessment of internal controls

405 Exemption

406 Code of ethics for senior financial officers

407 Disclosure of audit committee financial expert

408 Enhanced review of periodic disclosures by issuers

409 Real-time issuer disclosures

In addition to the U.S. Sarbanes-Oxley Act, other countries have adopted, or are in the process of adopting, rules and regulations similar to specific aspects of the Act within their own markets and regulatory environments. It is too soon to determine how extensive these actions will be.

Summary

- Management of financial risk is vital for the existence of the international financial system. A number of initiatives are underway to better manage these risks.

- The risk of a failure of one or more counterparties is being addressed with new initiatives in settlement systems to reduce the potential for harm. The intention is that even a major default would not necessarily result in a systemic reaction between market participants.

- International central banks and regulators are building on an important framework for the stability of the international financial system. Enhanced capital adequacy standards, such as the Basel II Accord, are designed to provide additional protection against a major financial event, thus improving financial risk management globally.

Notes

i ISDA Margin Survey 2004.

ii The Act can be viewed at the Securities and Exchange Commission Web site at www.sec.gov.

Appendix

The following is a brief selection of resources and additional information that may be useful to readers, including associations, accounting and regulatory bodies, payment and settlement systems, central banks, and exchanges.

Associations

Global Association of Risk Professionals	www.garp.com
Professional Risk Managers International Association	www.prmia.org
International Swaps and Derivatives Association	www.isda.org
Bank for International Settlements	www.bis.org
Treasury Management Association of Canada	www.tmac.ca
Association of Financial Professionals	www.afponline.org
Association of Corporate Treasurers	www.treasurers.org
Futures Industry Association	www.faifii.org
British Bankers Association	www.bba.org.uk
Society for Worldwide Interbank Financial Telecommunication	www.swift.com

Accounting and Regulatory Bodies

Public Company Accounting Oversight Board	www.pcaobus.org
Financial Accounting Standards Board	www.fasb.org
International Accounting Standards Board	www.iasb.org
Accounting Standards Board Canada	www.acsbcanada.org
American Institute of Certified Public Accountants	www.aicpa.org

Commodity Futures Trading Commission   www.cftc.gov
U.S. Securities and Exchange Commission   www.sec.gov

Payment and Settlement Systems

Clearing House Interbank Payment System   www.chips.org
Continuous Linked Settlement   www.cls-group.com

Central Banks

U.S. Federal Reserve   www.federalreserve.gov
European Central Bank   www.ecb.int
Bank of Canada   www.bankofcanada.ca
Bank of England   www.bankofengland.co.uk

Exchanges

Chicago Mercantile Exchange   www.cme.com
Chicago Board of Trade   www.cbot.com
New York Board of Trade   www.nybot.com
New York Mercantile Exchange   www.nymex.com
Winnipeg Commodity Exchange   www.wce.com
London Metals Exchange   www.lme.com
The International Petroleum Exchange   www.theipe.com
Euronext.Liffe   www.liffe.com
EUREX   www.eurexchange.com
Chicago Climate Exchange   www.chicagoclimateexchange.com

Credit Rating Agencies

Dominion Bond Rating Service Limited (DBRS)   www.dbrs.com
Fitch, Inc.   www.fitchratings.com
Moody's Investors Service, Inc.   www.moodys.com
Standard & Poor's Ratings Services (S&P)   www.standardandpoors.com

Index